HUNGER FOR HOPE

"If you've ever thought you don't have what it takes to make a difference in your own life and the lives of others, read *Hunger for Hope*. Ricardo Pierre-Louis tells his story of how God used the game of soccer, a series of circumstances, and people in his path to guide him to a life of leadership, empowerment, and service. He proves that one person, no matter how humble their beginnings, really can change the world. *Hunger for Hope* is well-written, interesting, and powerfully inspirational! Ricardo shows us what Christ meant when He answered the question, "Who is my neighbor?"

Kevin Cramer
United States Senator, North Dakota

"*Hunger for Hope* is an inspiring and fascinating look at the life of an extraordinary young athlete and leader. Ricardo was a star on the soccer field, but this fast-moving account of his life is even more remarkable than his athletic skills. It is honestly hard to put down; it's a terrific book!"

Dr. Charles Paul Conn
Chancellor, Lee University

"When, as in the case of Ricardo Pierre-Louis and soccer, his passion is also his job, reading this book means getting to know happiness. Ricardo's intelligence comes from his recognition of his unique ability to spread joy through his sport. He has hope to share! This book is proof that man does not live by bread alone."

Patrice Dumont
Senator, Haiti

"*Hunger for Hope* will shape your perspective regarding the possibilities of growth and development for children living in poverty. Intertwined throughout this story, Ricardo Pierre-Louis has captured his love of life, love of God, love of family, love of country, and love of opportunity. If sport and stories of dreams come true are dear to your heart, this book will certainly uplift your spirit."

Steve Madler
Principal, Century High School

"I am impressed with the message of perseverance in this book. Growing up with so few material items, the love that is shown in someone's life is so much more important in setting goals, persevering, and not giving up. More important than himself are those that Ricardo has encouraged along the way."

Kevin Reisenauer
Supervisor & Marketing Education Advisor,
DECA & Collegiate DECA

"Ricardo's story is also my story. I am very proud to have found myself in this book, and be a part of Ricardo's journey. Have a look and you will find yourself, too."

Jean-Jacques Pierre
Head Coach, Haiti National Soccer Team

"Hunger for Hope serves as an inspiring account where the threads of soccer, education, and spiritual gratitude are woven throughout Ricardo's journey. Truly, it is a humble honor to know and work alongside Ricardo as he serves as a model coach, educator, and man of faith whose mission is to make a difference for individuals, change the trajectory of families, and work to redefine communities here in Bismarck and in his native Haiti."

Dr. Ben Johnson
Assistant Superintendent, Bismarck Public Schools

"The story of Ricardo's rise from the impoverished streets of Haiti to international soccer star is truly inspiring, not only to Haitians but to anyone dreaming of a better life through Christ. I've been honored to join Ricardo on his mission through Lespwa Lavi and witness the power of God firsthand. Ricardo faith, vision, and generosity continue to amaze me."

Dr. Kadon Hintz
Director of Emergency Medicine, Sanford Health - Bismarck

"Hunger for Hope is a compelling glimpse into another culture, perseverance in life, and of course soccer... lots of soccer! I was amazed by the personal stories that kept me reading and rooting for the author as he became a world class athlete and human being. What an inspiring story. This is a must read!"

Dr. Tabby Rabenberg
Principal, Horizon Middle School

"*Hunger for Hope* is not only a soccer story, but a story of how a child's hunger for food led him to a sport that would change his life, and the lives of other children, forever. This is a story of a child who was fed with hope far more often than with food. Today, Ricardo is a hope giver and a dream maker. As a teacher and soccer coach in my school and district, I could not be more proud of all he has accomplished for himself and his family."

Tom Schmidt
Principal, Legacy High School

"The hard work and determination of Ricardo Pierre-Louis throughout his life, and his desire now to feed and educate Haitian children, is an inspiration to anyone in this land of plenty."

Kris Cramer
Wife of Senator Kevin Cramer

"Ricardo's success on the soccer field has been matched by his success off of it. His story shows the importance of faith, family, and resilience throughout life's journey. These experiences show why Ricardo is able to be so successful as a teacher and coach."

David Wisthoff
Principal, Bismarck High School

HUNGER FOR HOPE

MY REMARKABLE JOURNEY FROM POVERTY TO HAITIAN SOCCER STAR

BY

RICARDO PIERRE-LOUIS

ISBN: 978-1-7344222-9-0

Published by **STORY** ⑈ **CHORUS**

DEDICATION

To the memory of my father Odilon Joseph Pierre-Louis.

Today, as a parent myself, I see so clearly the love, hard work, dedication, commitment, and self-sacrifices my parents made for me. Being a parent makes me appreciate my own parents so much more.

My father passed away unexpectedly in February of 2020, while I was writing this book. He was only sixty-eight years old. The night before he died he was playing the accordion and dancing in the streets of Léogâne. He went home feeling ill, was rushed to the hospital that night, and died of a hernia complication. It shocked and devastated us all.

As I wrote this book in the months after he died, I was always thinking of him in a special way.

I remember how he worked from sunup to sundown driving a tap tap, earning twenty-five cents a day on a good day, to feed me and send me to school. I remember how he was always proud of me for every small bit of success. My father never missed any of my soccer games in Haiti. He went to games where it took him three days to get there, walking and hitchhiking. He traveled everywhere I played, from the time I was thirteen until the end of my career. I remember the way he taught me to be an entrepreneur despite his informal education background.

I remember his passion for music, his love for people, and his desire to help others. Although my father is no longer here, I feel his impact every day of my life.

Papa, even though you couldn't read or write, you are the author of this book.

> *"This book is for you, Papa. As a father who gave himself up for his children, you embodied the love of Jesus Christ in so many ways: in compassion, agape, and superhuman self-sacrifice. You were well-loved everywhere you went. As you look down from heaven, I hope you're proud of your little boy."*

TABLE OF CONTENTS

FOREWORD

Have you ever been in a room with someone great without realizing you're in the presence of greatness? I'm a little embarrassed to admit that I spent weeks in the same room with Ricardo before I discovered the parts of his story he has now made available to you in this book.

After someone shared part of Ricardo's story with me, I quickly searched his name online and discovered so many things I hadn't known before, including his soccer accolades on a collegiate, national, and professional level. This acquaintance of mine was accomplished as a player, as a coach, and as a professional in his career.

Yet, as I've come to know Ricardo more, I've discovered that his accolades, while significant, are not the greatest components of who he is. His greatness is in the quality of his character, the sincerity of his Christian faith, and the conviction in his spirit. He is a quality husband, father, friend, and role model. And most recently, Ricardo's faith and conviction have caused him to become an innovative and committed humanitarian and entrepreneur.

Ricardo has an uncommon love, care, and compassion for people. His personal experiences motivate him to create a better life for those around him. Through Magic Soccer, Lespwa Lavi, and as a teacher and coach, Ricardo has focused on the next generation, made up of many who are looking for the same assistance and opportunities that Ricardo sought when he was a child. Many strive to be great or to be better, but Ricardo uses his greatness to make our world better.

We live in a world that is desperate for hope. The calamities of starvation, poverty, social injustice, and lack of opportunity are devastating. These realities cause a reaction within each of us. We can lose hope. We can turn a blind eye. We can do nothing.

Or, we can reach for hope. We can provide hope.

Ricardo's story will grip your heart. The realities of his childhood, the challenges he's faced, and his hope for the future will change how you see the world. But his hope for you is not just that you'd be impacted. His hope is that by being impacted, you will decide to go make an impact. That, like Ricardo, you'll be inspired by what could be—by hope—and that his story will be a catalyst for you to change your story, and the story of those around you.

I love my friend Ricardo. I am incredibly honored to know him. I am so grateful he has put his story into words so you can know him too.

Josh Skjoldal
Lead Pastor
Evangel Church - Bismarck, ND

PREFACE

Mesaj sa pou tout Ayisyen, tout frèm yo, tout sèm yo! Lespwa se yon bagay pwisan. Li enspire nou pou nou fè enposib la epi li ede nou kontinye nan moman difisil yo. Lespwa ka vini sou anpil fason diferan ak anpil fòm diferan . Li ka nan mizik nou pi renmen an, nan foubòl, oswa yon bon liv, oswa menm koute pawòl lidè ou panse ki pi renmen nou an. Se konsa, si w'ap chèche pou yon ti kras enspirasyon yon ti bagay siplemantè, ou te vini dwat nan bon plas la. Kisa Tousen tap di, tap fè sil tap viv nan eta Haiti ye jounen jodia? Pwoblèm yo komplike, men solisyon yo senp. Li lè, li tan pou nou pran aksyon, li lè li tan pou nou sispan espere, li lè li tan pou nou viv vi zansèt nou yo te pwojekte pou nou an.

LIV SA SE AVNI AYISYEN PARÈY MWEN, AVNI PEYI MWEN.

LIV SA A SE KÒMANSMAN CHANJMAN NAN AYITI NOU RENMEN ANPIL LA.

This message is for all Haitians! Hope is a powerful thing. It inspires us to do the impossible and helps us continue in difficult times. Hope can come in many different forms. It can be in our favorite music, in soccer, a good book, or even listening to the words of your favorite leader. So if you're looking for a little extra little inspiration, you've come to the right place. What would Toussaint say if he was living in Haiti today? Problems are complicated, but solutions are simple. It's time to take action, it's time to stop hoping, it's time to live the life our ancestors wanted for us.

This book is the future of my fellow Haitians, the future of my country.

This book is the beginning of change in our beloved Haiti.

Ricardo

INTRODUCTION

If not for soccer, my life would be different.

You would never pick up a book and read about my life, because a book about me would not exist. Like most people from my home country of Haiti, soccer has always occupied much of my mind. It's more than a hobby or something that young people do for fun. It's more than exercise. It's more than a career.

There's a secret you may not know.

If you grew up in Haiti, you would understand perfectly.

You would view soccer so differently, and you'd begin to see the packed stadiums and dusty street matches for what they were: People reaching out for opportunity for themselves, their families, and their communities.

In Haiti, soccer is hope and life itself. It's the door to a better future. It's all about opportunity. It goes far beyond the game at hand.

When you understand this, you'll be ready to change the world.

Because soccer was never just a game.

CHAPTER ONE

SAVE MY SUNDAY

The fate of my city rested on one kick.

It was the last match of the season, the big game against FICA du Cap-Haïtien, who were our rivals from the north coast of Haiti. The crowds in my city of Léogâne were fervently hoping for a win, placing all the responsibility on our team, Cavaly.

Sometimes, you look for the glory of the championship, but this match was different. It wasn't just about a win, or a trophy. There was more riding on this.

Cap-Haïtien *[Kap-Ay-is-yen]* was a Goliath. They were the defending league champions, and their team had some of Haiti's top scoring players including Golman Pierre, who had set the single season scoring record in the 2001-2002 season with 24 goals. They had a history of sending players to the Haitian National Team and beyond. Cavaly *[Kav-a-li]*, on the other hand, had lost Daniel Mentor, Clamart Augustin, Sammuel Dalcé, our three best players, the year before. We were like David, armed with just a few stones, a lot of hope, and the will to fight—not just to win, but to stay alive.

It's easy to dismiss soccer as just a game, but in Haiti, losing and placing in the bottom three positions meant we would be removed from the top division of the Haitian Professional League and placed into the second division. We called that second division *hell*.

In the second division, lost sponsorships and lack of money meant some teams would cease to exist. No one wanted to play for a second division team. There are no opportunities and very little chance of making the national team. Playing in the second division meant that hope for the opportunities soccer offered were all but gone. We understood that if we won, we would get money to live and buy food. If we lost, we would not.

It wasn't just about us, though, and the fans knew it. Not only would our players and their families suffer from a move down to the second division, but the whole city would be hurt too. What happened to Cavaly happened to Léogâne [*Ley-o-gàn*].

The pressure we felt that day was intense, like no other match I've ever played, before or since. There was no room for error, because losing meant a loss for everyone in my city.

THE WEIGHT OF SILENCE

The team rushed into the stadium from the tunnel, and we saw the crowd on their feet chanting and screaming, tossing red smoke bombs onto the field to show support for our team. Our eyes watered as we pushed through the smoke and onto the field, our red jerseys standing out from the bright yellow and green shirts of Cap-Haïtien.

The coin toss, the opening kick, and then, within minutes, Cap-Haïtien scored.

All of the energy and hope we'd mustered for the match immediately shifted to defensively fighting for our lives for the next 45 minutes. We were so nervous that we weren't playing well at all, and as the match went on, the crowd slowly grew quieter.

At halftime, the stadium was silent, and some in the crowd could be seen praying. Our coach, who was visibly crying, did not let us go into the locker room out of fear that giving us that rest would lessen our resolve to win.

The second half of the match went just as badly. Cap-Haïtien played well, though they did not score. Miraculously, our goalkeeper somehow kept them from scoring, and many of their shots sent the ball bouncing back after striking the goal post. Yet as a team, the pressure of the game and what was at stake had made us afraid to be aggressive, and we put nothing on the scoreboard. It seemed as if all our hope was disappearing, like the time left on the clock.

The weight of the closing minutes were so heavy I could almost feel it. I remembered reading about Brazil's 1950 World Cup final, known as The Maracanazo, or The Agony of Maracanã, where a few people had committed suicide over the loss. I did not want to lose for any reason, especially knowing that for some fans in the thousands watching and listening, the outcome could be grim. I prayed for the Lord to help us.

With just a few minutes left, and little hope of scoring a goal to tie and stay alive in the first division, one of our players was knocked down and we were awarded a penalty kick.

The crowd came back to life with a roar.

A tiny, terrified spark of hope had ignited them. It seemed as if God had actually given us a chance. Whether or not we would stay in the first division rested on one kick. Yet no one on my team wanted to take that kick.

If you failed, the blame would be all on you. All the anger and disappointment of the team and the city would rest on you. You would be the one place they could focus their disappointment and anger, and it would be so bad that you would have to move away, or risk having your home burned down, or even being killed. The realization of the situation set in, and just as quickly as the excitement had washed over the stadium, tension flooded back into the fans and our team. The coach motioned to Jackson Dalce, one of our most experienced players, and as he took the ball, many in the crowd turned away. Even our coach covered his eyes and started to pray. It was nearly unbearable to watch.

There was silence.

The referee blew the whistle.

There was the soft thud of a foot meeting the ball, and then... the ball was in the back of the net.

We had scored.

The stadium exploded in noise, almost as if a bomb went off. People were crying and screaming, turning to those next to them and hugging each other. You could hear the sound of the celebration across the city. We defended that tie for the remaining moments of the match, knowing that we had saved our place in the first division. We'd played for our life, and we'd kept it for another year.

ARRIVE EARLY AND WAIT

I grew up in Léogâne, a city with a population of ninety thousand, just nineteen miles west of Port-au-Prince, the capital of Haiti. It is a warm city, both in climate and in culture. Léogâne sits on the coast of the Port-au-Prince Bay, the coastal plains a rich green, full of sugar cane and other crops, with hills to the south. It is mostly known today as the epicenter of the devastating 2010 earthquake, which left much of the city's buildings and infrastructure in ruins. Léogâne is culturally rich with music and celebration and delicious cuisine, but it is economically poor. Soccer has always served as a source of pride and focus that the community could come together around, just as it is for every Haitian city. We can always come together for our team and hope for success alongside our players.

That's because in Haiti, there's a different church most people go to on Sundays. That church might have a crowd of twenty thousand or more, hoping and pleading for success before the altar. It is a faith like no other, one where the altar is a net and the church is the soccer field.

SOCCER IS LIKE A RELIGION IN HAITI, AND THE PLAYERS ARE LIKE GODS.

Two days before every match, the crowds begin forming, lining up outside the stadium and settling in for the wait. The stadium in Léogâne was built to hold about twelve thousand people, but would ultimately have more than twice that once the match began. You could buy a ticket, but having one meant nothing. More tickets were sold than seats were available, and if you wanted into the stadium, you had better arrive early and wait.

The muffled noise of the growing crowd could be heard during those two days leading up to the match. Blaring trumpets and thudding tom-tom drums, cheers and chants and songs, even arguments about how the match would go; this was our pre-game music. You could smell the smoke from cooking food, though on match day, many wouldn't eat until it was over, because their stomachs would be too nervous during the match.

Radios were very important, since most families did not have televisions. Those who couldn't get in the stadium to see the match would listen to it on the radio. Imagine an entire city coming to life with shouts and horns, all at the same time. When the stadium erupted with the screams of the fans, the city did as well, the noise stretching over the buildings and into the hills as each play was broadcast over the air and into every radio.

Smoke bombs and streamers would rain down on us as we played. Our soccer matches were wild and chaotic. Everything was about the match in the stadium. Everyone wanted in. Everyone wanted to know what happened there. All focus rested on one place. All hope and imagination was set there.

As a child, it was not easy to get into a soccer match. On match day, people climbed into the trees or on high buildings, hoping to see into the stadium. Children who did not have a ticket, but were desperate to get in, showed up on the day of the match and begged arriving players to take them inside, grabbing their hands, grasping for a chance to see the match. Even though my parents would punish me for it, I was often there as a child. I wanted to get into the stadium because soccer equals opportunity in Haiti, and I wanted to be a part of it.

NOTHING IS NORMAL

Growing up, I had about three items of clothing that I would alternate wearing. On washing day, my mother would gather all of our clothes and walk six miles to the river. We would not wear clothes that day. She worked very hard, but she did not have much education. Her parents were not able to afford school, and so she could not read or write, even her own name.

Each morning my father would leave at 5:00 a.m. to drive a tap tap, a brightly painted vehicle used as a taxi. He did not own the vehicle, and so the owner would keep 90 percent of the daily profits. My father would bring home the rest of the money at night.

Nearly every child in Haiti knows that you are not guaranteed to eat each day, and it was no different for me. There were times my father didn't arrive home in time with the day's earnings, so my mother would not have money to buy food for my two sisters, my brother, and me. On those nights, my mother would walk two miles to the market in the dark, with me and one of my sisters holding onto her skirt, to sell firewood and water. If she made twenty-five cents, she'd buy us bread to eat. That bread might be our only meal that day.

My parents worked very hard, and my mother was good at finding ways to make money. We were surviving one day at a time. But then, in the 1990s, the trade embargo hit Haiti.

In 1991, when I was around six years old, a military coup removed Haiti's elected president, Jean-Bertrand Aristide. Soon after, the United Nations urged its members to impose a trade embargo on Haiti. The effect was devastating. People lost their jobs and unemployment was rampant. We struggled in every aspect of our daily lives. There was very little gas, which had an impact on tap tap drivers like my father. My family, like many others, had little access to food. We would eat whatever we could, and there were times I would eat only raw mangoes and ketchup.

SOMETIMES WE HAD TO EAT DIRT TO STAY ALIVE.

My mother would mix mud with a little salt, bake it, and we would eat it. Or she would give us salt and water to fill our stomachs. It helped with low blood pressure and took away the radiating feeling of hunger, because hunger is very hard to manage physically. Your stomach hurts. It bubbles and growls. The very center of your body is in pain. It makes you lightheaded and so tired that you have a difficult time staying awake. Once you reach your maximum capacity for pain, mentally, you can get used to hunger, but the physical realities eventually take a toll. Like a habit, hunger is something I went through over and over, and it became a normal state of being.

My parents tried very hard. I know it was difficult for them to hear us say that we were hungry when there was nothing they could feed us. They could not open the cupboard and give us a snack. And so, my mother fed us with hope. She would tell us there would be food in a few hours, or she would find ways to calm the hunger pangs.

During this embargo period, there was also a nightly curfew. We were not allowed to go out after curfew, so there was the sense that we weren't in control of our own lives. Fear of invasion, due to the military coup, led many people to dig holes in the ground to hide in, just in case bombs might be dropped by some invading country. The sound of shooting was common, and we existed on the edge of constant hunger and violence. Nothing felt normal. I remember that part of my childhood as being incredibly difficult.

SEEING OPPORTUNITY

In 1994, Aristide was returned to power and troops from several countries, led by the United States, arrived in Haiti. Things slowly began to change for the better after the embargo was lifted.

The American soldiers who arrived were a special memory for me. They would give children rides around in their tanks, and we loved the soldiers because they were kind to us. They would play with us, which was unusual. Our own fathers often did not have time to play with us, because they were working so much, trying to support their families. And so we loved to play with the soldiers, appreciating the attention they gave us. We didn't know much English, so all we could really say was "Hey you! Hey you! Give me one dollar!"

It is strange to consider that, until those soldiers came to Haiti, I had never seen a white person before. We'd touch their hair, which was so different from ours, and be in awe of them. We had heard about Jesus, but really didn't know much about him. All we knew is that Jesus meant hope, and I actually thought those white people were Jesus.

My grandmother lived in Canada, and it was then, after the embargo lifted, that things began to slowly change for my family. She was able to send my family some money, as well as a freezer and a black-and-white television. That freezer became more than just an appliance or a convenience for our family. My mother, who had an entrepreneurial spirit, saw it as an opportunity.

Haiti is a tropical climate, and can be very hot. My mother saw the opportunity to use the little money we had, and our new freezer, to begin making popsicles to sell to people looking for a cold treat. Each morning she would fill plastic bags with natural fruit juices and freeze them for the next day. She quickly grew her popsicle business by seeing it as a chance to help others.

We weren't the only ones who had gone hungry, you see.

There were so many others in our neighborhood who were struggling to eat, so she hired them. They helped pack the popsicles and sell them, using portable coolers filled with salt. She would give them one hundred popsicles to sell, and twenty would be theirs after they sold eighty. She did not need to pressure them to sell what they were given for the day; they were motivated by the need to make money. Her entrepreneurial spirit influenced many in the community, including my siblings and myself.

In the following years, as her popsicle business continued to bring in some money, my mother also began to cook food for both our family and her workers to eat. She was a very good cook, and that skill eventually grew into a small restaurant business. Each day she would get up very early, getting the popsicles doled out, and then preparing the meals for the restaurant. She worked hard to feed as many people as she could.

Hunger is a motivator, you see.

It helps you see opportunity more clearly.

A mother will do just about anything to make sure her family has food to eat. My mother would look at every situation and weigh it to see what kind of opportunity it was, and whether it could solve our most pressing problems.

In the midst of poverty and all the problems our people face, those who live outside Haiti might consider it foolish to talk about how much hope and excitement came with every soccer match. It may seem strange to give so much attention to this sport, instead of church or education. But when you realize how much opportunity is tied up in the game of soccer, you start to understand this "religion" of Haiti.

CHAPTER TWO

LIFE IS A COMPETITION

When you were three, were you competing for your future?

Most three-year-olds aren't planning their future, but in Haiti, that future can depend on how well you do in kindergarten. Because of that, children begin preparation for the rest of their lives when they are just toddlers.

Children in Haiti have many burdens placed on them that are not common in other countries. They work hard to help their family survive from a young age. They learn to cope with limited food and clean water. And, starting at age three, they learn to compete for their education.

To gain entry into a Catholic school in Haiti, the only decent education available, students must pass a test. At age three, children start preparing for the test that they will take around age five. The test, which is oral, determines how well a child can identify colors and numbers, among other skills. There's also an IQ test. We weren't promised an education, we had to earn it.

Families who could afford the expense would hire tutors for their young children. The children would take paid classes and lessons for two and a half years of preparation.

My family could not afford a good tutor.

This was not uncommon, but my parents knew how important it was for me to do well on the test. They wanted me to get into the Catholic school so I could have a better future than they had. My parents were able to hire someone who lived on our street, and had graduated from high school, to tutor me. This was better than nothing, but my older sister who also lived in Canada at the time, knew I would need more help. She wanted me to receive tutoring to better my chances at success, so she sent money to my mother to pay for classes during my final summer before the test. Despite the fact that my sister lived in a tiny apartment and worked two jobs to make ends meet, she knew how important my education was, and sent all she could.

The kids whose families could afford it had two and a half years of paid tutoring going into the test. I had only one summer.

The tutoring class was busy, a way for the Catholic school to make money. It was like a revolving door of kids coming and going all day, and a reminder that there were so many students trying for very few openings at the school.

Tests were administered in May. And whether I was successful or not, the test itself would cost my parents money. Both my mother and I had to dress very nice on the day of the test, so she bought me new long socks, dress shoes, a purple and gray shirt, and gray shorts. I was so proud to wear my new clothes on test day.

The test wasn't the only thing being graded. How we looked mattered. The school took the image of the parents into account when selecting students because their goal was to choose the best of the best. Behavior, appearance, and knowledge were all part of the test.

My first job interview, essentially, was at age five.

NO SCHOOL, NO OPPORTUNITY

What happened on test day would determine if I would receive an education or not, and even at age five, I was very aware of the importance of the moment. My parents had made it clear that if I wanted to be like them, struggling to earn enough money while working hard all day, I could go ahead and fail. If I wanted a better chance in life, I had to do well.

My father, especially, took this very seriously. We like to think of parents or mentors working with children out of a passion for learning and an enthusiasm for their personal growth, but this is somewhat the opposite with Haitian parents. There is much more riding on the test. The pressure to make this one, solitary moment count for everything was a lot to bear. On the day of the test, my father knelt down in front of me with tears in his eyes, and with a forceful voice practically yelled at me, "This is your chance, your only chance in life. Don't waste it."

Up until the day he died many decades later, my father could not read or write, and he desperately wanted something different for me. He was so afraid to see history repeat itself. His worry fed my own.

All of this, at five years old.

My mother and I walked just over two miles to the school for the test, and took our seats on benches lining the walls. There were many parents and children there. It felt like a doctor's office, a mix of anxiety and nerves, where everything seems a little intimidating. The testing building was much different than anything I knew, and the test was administered by a white priest.

I think now of how overwhelming that day should have been, with so many foreign experiences and all of the pressure. I could easily have let the pressure get the best of me. Yet I remember feeling confident in those strange surroundings, even though the competition was fierce. Imagine all of the five-year-olds in a city of ninety thousand, competing for one of only sixty available openings.

When the test was over, my mother and I walked home. My new clothes were put away.

We waited a month for the test results. School would start in September, and we wouldn't know my fate until June. The school would post a list of all of the children who had passed, meaning everyone could see who succeeded and who did not. If your name was on the list, you were accepted into the school. When the day came and the list was posted, word spread quickly around town. We rushed to the school, and my parents pushed their way through a crowd of people to see the list.

My name was on it.

My parents were so happy that their son had made it into school that they began to cry. They lifted me up and celebrated, shouting and cheering, proud to let everyone know. Later, as a special treat for my success, I was given extra food to eat. Food is a good reward for a child used to going hungry.

Being accepted into school was only the first challenge though. There were yearly expenses, such as new uniforms, which were required to attend school. I would be fed at school, but that wasn't free either. My parents didn't have the money for much of these additional expenses, so my sister continued sending money from Canada to help pay for these things. She wanted me to stay in school.

Along with the financial challenges that went with staying in school, students faced extreme social pressure and possibly humiliation based on how well we performed at school. It is not a stretch to say that what happened with these tests, and what happened to you in school at a young age, would absolutely determine your life in Haiti. How you handled the stress and competition that existed in Haitian schools would form who you were.

Consider my younger brother, who took the test two years after I did, but did not pass. He ended up going to a low-level school that my parents still had to pay for him to attend. Most days he would hide at school to avoid getting beaten for getting answers wrong, which caused him to fall further and further behind, and eventually drop out. To this day, my brother drives a truck in Haiti and only has a second grade education. That might not seem so bad, but years later, he was unable to immigrate to Canada with the rest of the family because of his poor education.

IN HAITI, YOUR LIFE IS A CONSTANT COMPETITION.

You don't get to the next rung of the ladder without a fight.

THE FEAR OF PUNISHMENT

Getting to my school was about a two-mile walk, and that walk had to fit into a busy work-centered family schedule. Sometimes, when I was young, my father would dress me and walk me to school before returning home to get to work. Walking to school with my father is a favorite memory of mine.

He would hold my hand and smile widely as we walked the two miles. My father didn't smile often, but seeing me in my school uniform made him happy. My chance at an education was one of his biggest accomplishments, and he would tell me over and over how proud he was of me.

The classroom and schoolwork were not easy, and it took me a while to get used to the pressure that went with the system. The directors of the school were white, and they took their job seriously. My teachers did not mess around either, and they used fear as a motivator.

1 John 4:18 says that fear is directly tied to punishment, and I can say this is true from what I experienced at school early on. Students were so afraid to speak up or interrupt class that they didn't even want to ask if they could use the restroom. Instead, they would try to hold it until lunch. Many times, they couldn't. Kids would pee on themselves and, humiliated, were sent to the janitor. If they had made a big mess of themselves, they were moved somewhere private and forced to sit naked.

We knew that the teachers would hit us, even if we gave the right answers. We knew that we could be humiliated if we didn't do our homework. Fear kept us in line.

We were required to maintain a set GPA, and each week we were ranked from 1–60. By second grade, it was 1–55, because each year the class lost students who couldn't keep up. Each year during the seven years of primary school, the directors would choose the top three students and present them in front of everyone. I managed to always be in the top ten in my first years of school and, as the years went on, I was always in the top five. I wanted to succeed, and had the motivation to do so.

Everything was public, both the reward and the humiliation. Students knew they were competing with each other, with their classmates and friends. Those with the highest GPA rank sat in the back of the class, creating a hierarchy that couldn't be ignored.

COMPETITION AMONG FRIENDS

Our class days were rigidly structured. We said the pledge of allegiance to Haiti and raised the flag. We had to be respectful, or else we would be disciplined. We were required to go to church at the Cathedral every Sunday. If we missed church, we couldn't go to school the next Monday, and our parents would have to come to the school and explain our absence. If the reason wasn't acceptable or we missed too much church, we could be kicked out of school. The cloud that hung over everything—from grades to attendance to classroom obedience—was the fear of losing all the opportunities we had worked toward.

This competition and discipline had a measurable effect. By the time I reached seventh grade, there were only thirty-six students out of the original sixty.

You might wonder why anyone would want to go to school with this kind of environment. But at school, I was able to eat.

Every day, we each brought our own bowl to school in our backpacks for the two meals the school would provide. Some days we ate cooked wheat with a meatless sauce. The other days might be a bowl of flour with beans for protein. We were often given a simple piece of plain bread, or a gourd, as another meal. We had to pay a little for the food, but it was still good that we were able to get a regular meal at least once a day.

I went to school from 7:30 a.m. to 4:30 p.m. each day. That meant that during some months of the year, it would be dark by the time I got home, and I often struggled with doing my homework by candlelight. Homework was challenging enough on its own, with hours of memorization from many different books. We had to do recitations the next day, so skipping my homework wasn't an option. The stress over the homework would sometimes upset my stomach so much that I would not be able to eat until I was finished. Other evenings, I did not eat at all, because my parents had not returned and there was no food.

So much revolved around food. Hunger was an ongoing battle, and because of school, I usually ate two meals a day. I would do anything to stay in school.

Over time, I began to understand the schooling system and found ways to exist in it, and even enjoy it. School began to be a fun place. At one point, I had a teacher, Maitre Clermont Coimin, who was a soccer player, and I would go to watch him play on Sundays.

IN FACT, IT WAS BECAUSE OF SCHOOL THAT I GOT MY FIRST TASTE OF SOCCER.

After the first school meal, we would get a fifteen-minute recess. When I was around twelve years old, I started to play soccer with friends during those recesses.

Once I took to playing soccer at school, my friends and I tried to get a game going every chance we could. We'd set up games between different grades, and rush out to the field near the school to play for the fifteen wonderful minutes we were allotted each break. I wasn't what anyone would consider a good soccer player, but I had fun.

Between those small soccer breaks was a time of serious schoolwork.

Since the spirit of competition was so strong at school, we learned how to trick each other for our own benefit. If another student hadn't done their lessons for the afternoon session, I would try to get them involved in a game of soccer or tag. That way, instead of studying, they would spend their noon break playing, not be prepared for class, and I would come out ahead that day. My classmates and friends would do that same thing to me or anyone else.

It might seem strange that I would trick my friends into getting lower grades so that I could succeed, but these tactics were how students avoided being left behind in their education.

This was the only system we knew.

THERE IS NOT ENOUGH

Around 1800, as the Haitian revolution was ongoing, Toussaint Louverture fought to end slavery and begin educating enslaved Haitians and their children. The first schooling provided to Haitians began in 1801, but out of a fear that the enslaved people would become "too smart", the French asked the Catholic Church to come in and create schools that would educate only a handful of people. Fathers had to be in the army, and women were not allowed to attend school. Even today in Haiti, there are a limited number of government schools, and most schools are privately run.

The schooling put in place was a classical education system based heavily on French curriculum. The children of enslaved Haitians were forced to compete against the enslavers' children for the opportunity to go to university in France. The system was built on educating only the best and brightest, and forcing everyone else out. Unfortunately, that same classical educational system exists in Haiti today.

It is a system with a ceiling; limitations are purposely built in. You can claw your way through every level of education and learn all you can from the system, but at some point there is nowhere else to go. Unless you are one of a very lucky few who go on to university, you are stuck under that ceiling.

There is no sympathy for children who have any disadvantages. Those with anxiety or learning disabilities are just left behind. Young girls are likely to remain uneducated, and instead are expected to stay home to do chores and housework. They are mostly seen as worthless.

This brutal education system is built on centuries of holding the Haitian people down and forcing them to compete with each other for what little there is. When I was in school, I was constantly competing with everyone, even close friends. I looked for any opportunity to slow down my top classmates, knowing they were the fiercest gladiators in the arena.

Remember, where I'm from there is not enough food for everyone. There is not enough clean water for everyone. There are not enough educational opportunities for everyone.

You have to compete for these basic needs.

The same entry test that I took as a five-year-old has existed since 1801, when enslaved children were first allowed to compete for schooling.

This is why only about 50 percent of children ever attend school. And less than 2 percent graduate.

This is still the system today.

CHAPTER THREE

TAKING ROOT

When I was around twelve years old and nearing the end of seventh grade, I was in front of my mother's restaurant kicking around a tennis ball. I had come to enjoy soccer and kicking a ball around, but that was where it ended for me. I never dreamed soccer would be anything more in my life.

I gave the ball a hard kick with my left foot and watched it sail down the street. A man spoke up from behind me.

Apollon was a customer of my mother's, often eating at her restaurant. He'd seen me kick the ball.

"You remind me of the Brazilian soccer star, Roberto Carlos," he said.

I was flattered but surprised. He encouraged me to join a street soccer team that he coached. Street teams are unorganized soccer, but most great players from my country have had their start there. The streets where Apollon's team played weren't paved, like many places in my town. They were dirt streets, with air that carried the strong smell of the nearby alcohol and shoe factories. Street soccer was crude and dangerous, but Apollon's street team played in one of the best street soccer tournaments in the area. I was thrilled that he had asked me to join his team.

No one had ever asked me to play soccer before in any kind of organized fashion. My soccer experience had been kicking the ball around with classmates from my primary school.

Street soccer might have been the lowest form of organized soccer, but that didn't mean it was unimportant. Street soccer tournaments in Haiti are so much more than neighborhood kids playing a fun game. There's just as much passion for the game in those small street tournaments than in any professional competition.

Just as cities were passionate about their teams, neighborhoods felt the same way about street soccer. People would stop what they were doing to watch the matches. It didn't matter if they were washing their clothes or feeding their kids. If you lived in the area, you found a way to watch, even if it meant going up on the roof to get a good view of the action.

The Christmas street soccer tournament was especially important in my town because it was a distraction from the everyday difficulties of survival. It gave people something to look forward to. Without something good in the future, all people can do is think about the struggles in their lives, which can become a negative downward spiral. But these small tournaments brought life and excitement to everyone. The soccer games gave them something they could rally around.

The enthusiastic crowd made up of our neighbors was what turned a simple street into a real arena for us. That crowd, packed tightly around the street's playing field, could get fierce and loud, cheering as the dust billowed around them. They made us players feel as if we were in a huge arena with fans cheering us on, and these matches would often go until dark.

Since street teams weren't a well-funded league team, the soccer ball would sometimes be a balloon with a sock pulled over it, tied with a string. A strong kick could send it flying or cause it to pop. We never had another balloon ball ready to go because the street soccer league couldn't afford extra balloons, which cost twenty cents from the store. Usually, if our balloon popped, spectators would chip in to buy another one to continue the game.

STREET SOCCER

I was eager to have a chance to play in the Christmas tournament, even though I had no real experience. Apollon told me that the match that day started at four. I hadn't told my parents I was playing street soccer because I knew they wouldn't approve. My parents were protective, and to play in the street soccer league, I had to go to the other side of town where they didn't want me to be. They knew what crowds at soccer matches were like and they believed the worst could happen.

I was tall and big for twelve years old, and that could have been a problem. The tournament officials didn't care so much about your age, but there were height limitations. When I showed up, there was an outcry that I was too big, too tall. I had to stand under a black charcoal mark that determined if players were too tall. Of course, I was just a tiny bit over the line. The officials made me push my back up against the wall to be sure I was standing straight. Back and forth it went as they determined if my height was acceptable. At one point, they actually cut my hair because it was making me too tall.

Here I was, fifteen minutes before the game was to start, and they were shaving my hair off to see if I made the height rules.

The officials finally relented, and I was on Apollon's tournament team. Street teams didn't have jerseys, of course. You either had a shirt on, or you didn't. We did have team names, though, and my new team's name was Kolorósh, which meant "clash of stone". I wasn't much of a player at that point. I could shoot the ball, but that was about it. Still, Apollon needed players on his team to simply fill it out, and so there I was, figuring things out as I went.

As the match began, I really did not know what I was doing, so I did what I knew I could. I shot the ball hard and ran fast. My team had the best player on the field, Louisino Garcon. He did everything for our team. It seemed like he was everywhere. To everyone's surprise we won 3-1. When it was over, people ran out into the street we were playing on to celebrate. They were throwing Louisino in the air and cheering for *us*, something I had never experienced before, and it was exciting.

At the game's end, we were filthy with dust and sweat. There was so much dirt in my eyes it was difficult to see. I knew I could not go home to my parents like that, so I tried to wash up in a nearby stream, even though it was dirty and full of factory runoff. Then I ran for home as quickly as I could, because my mother had no idea where I'd been.

> SOCCER WAS STARTING TO TAKE ROOT IN MY LIFE, BUT I WAS NOT AWARE THAT THIS PASSION WOULD CONTINUE TO GROW.

My education was still the most important thing to me and the only opportunity I saw for a better future.

WHAT MATTERS MORE?

Primary school ends after seventh grade for Haitian students. After that, in order to advance to secondary school, students have to pass the mandated government education test. If they don't pass, they don't enroll. As you can see, the system continued to narrow the funnel of who could progress onward.

I wasn't too concerned about passing the national test. The primary school I had been attending taught students at a high level. I had received an excellent education by Haitian standards, and students from my school were often in the top fifty when the regional testing results came in.

Yet, a great education in such a competitive, fear-based system has a steep price.

Remember what my life had been like since age five until the seventh grade. Each morning, I would get up early. I would go to school, where I would compete with the other students in order to get ahead. I would come home, and stay up late finishing homework by candlelight. It was without pause and left little room for anything else, including real friendships.

Many of my classmates were more like acquaintances than friends, and what was missing for me was the closeness most people experience and build in their years in school. It was strange, really, because I attended a Catholic school and we learned about Jesus Christ. We learned about his command to love each other, but the competitive environment at school made it difficult to live that out.

Wagner and Sebastien were the exceptions. They were my friends during those years, and are still some of my closest friends.

Wagner had a very high IQ, and I considered him to be the most intelligent in our class. He seemed to have more free time because studying wasn't as necessary for him, and many subjects at school came easier to him.

While we were spending our nights doing homework, Wagner was going to Protestant Christian crusades, which were large religious services dedicated to spreading the Christian faith in Haiti. He began learning about the Bible in a new way, a different way from what we were taught in Catholic school. Wagner brought what he had been learning to Sebastien and me.

"There has to be more," he said, referring to what we'd been doing the past seven years. At age twelve, our entire lives were wrapped around doing our best at school and competing with each other. We'd received a good education, Wagner said, but we needed to think more deeply about the things in life that actually mattered more than that.

He brought up how our actions often were not Christ-like, or even the behavior of a friend. "If we are tricking each other to get better grades, what good does it do?"

Wagner wanted us to go to crusade services with him, and spend less time on our classwork. He wanted us to hear the messages at the service, to learn what he was learning. Sebastien and I both wondered if this was yet another trick, another attempt to get ahead. Here he was, the smartest student out of all of us, apparently trying to convince us to study less.

"If you don't trust me," Wagner said, "just come once and you'll feel what I am talking about."

Wagner would not let up, and we finally agreed to go. Wagner said we would try to meet up at the service but there were going to be thousands of people there. So if we couldn't find each other, we would meet later to discuss what we had heard. He didn't want the seeds of our faith to fall on the ground without a chance to water them.

I remember that even as I approached the place where the services were, I could feel the difference. The singing was different from what I was used to at the Catholic church. The spirit of worship was different. The presence of God was so real I could almost feel it. I couldn't find Wagner or Sebastien, but I stood with the crowd before the stage and felt alive for the first time.

After attending that first crusade, Wagner, Sebastien, and I began to read the Bible for ourselves. While we had to memorize scripture and study catechisms for Catholic school, what we were reading in the Bible suddenly took on new meaning for us. Through these experiences, I became a true follower of Jesus Christ. The spiritual growth I was having in private was very different from the religious teachings I learned in school. I was still young, and I had a sense of fear about abandoning the religious path that I was familiar with. I memorized Psalm 23, "The Lord is my Shepherd..." and that became my favorite verse as I faced the unknown to come.

CONTINUING THE CLIMB

The summer after primary school ended, so did my habit of going to Catholic church on Sundays. It had become a habit because I was required to go to church for school. But since primary school was over, that requirement was gone.

Instead, I began to focus intently on God, praying directly to Him. I did not yet have my own Bible, or the resources to really grow in my newly found faith, but I began to feel hope for what was ahead.

In June, right after primary school graduation, I took three tests in one week for admittance to the three best secondary schools in our region, Saint Louis Gonzague *[Sen*

Lu-ee Gon-zag], Juvenat *[Ju-ven-a]*, and Lycée Anacaona de Léogâne *[Lee-say Ah-nah-cao-nah de Ley-o-gàn]*, all government schools. Each school had its own test, and I wanted to be sure I had options. If I didn't pass at least one of the tests, my education would be over.

There were private schools I could apply to, but they were not high quality. In Haiti, private secondary schools are usually worse than schools run by the government. The Haitian constitution says that everyone must have access to an education, which sounds very good, but it also allows anyone to open a school. There were very few restrictions on who could set up a school and the subjects they taught. Going to a private school might be a little better than no schooling, but for me, it would have been a failure.

My friends also took multiple tests around the same time. They had the same reasoning: Surely at least one of the tests will give us the opportunity we need. We waited for the results that would be released in July, trying not to worry.

I passed all three tests. My friends Wagner and Sebastien passed their tests as well.

This sounds like a win, as if we made it to the finish line. But just as with primary school, we had new problems. As usual, the question of money always made things difficult.

Going to Gonzague meant traveling to the wealthy section of Port-au-Prince. That would be an expensive commute every day. Juvenat, while a bit closer, still had a similar commute expense problem.

My parents worked hard, but we didn't have much money. My father's job as a tap tap driver and my mother's restaurant often paid for basic necessities, but there were still days when we went hungry. My mother made sure her paying restaurant customers ate, and if there was anything left, we ate as well. If she fed us first and customers couldn't eat, they would stop coming and her business would fail.

In comparison, Wagner's father had even less. He worked with my father as what's known as a hangman, someone who holds onto the side of a tap tap, fills the vehicle with gas, and yells for people to get in. On rides, he would hang off the side to avoid taking up a paying seat inside. He would try to fill the seats by playing into the idea that there weren't going to be available seats for long. As good as he was at it, there wasn't much income in that job. Our families wanted us to continue getting a good education, but being able to afford that was another story.

I very much wanted to go to Gonzague. It was almost painful because I'd tested well and the possibility was there, but we just could not afford it. I ended up going to Lycée Anacaona de Léogâne, the local school, because it was the only option we could pay for.

SCARCITY, WHETHER IN FOOD OR MONEY OR EDUCATIONAL OPPORTUNITIES, IS ALWAYS A DRIVING FORCE IN HAITI.

Think of the job of the hangman, creating pressure to get a seat in a tap tap by convincing you that there were more people than seats, and there was less and less time to get on board.

Act now! Limited time to take action! Limited seats! Not everyone will get something!

So much of the Haitian education system was built on that exact same idea. It's a constant competition against others, with kids always scrambling and grabbing for a seat. There are ladders leaning against all kinds of opportunity, but climbing those ladders ends up being a fight for each rung.

Much had changed since primary school. The world was getting a bit bigger, and my faith had begun to be an important part of my life.

So much change, and yet there was still something we could always count on being present, a thread that was woven through each day: hunger.

Hunger was still there, growling about inside. It was still a problem. When there's a problem, you constantly have your eyes out for a solution. As it turns out, hunger was what convinced me to continue playing soccer.

Hunger is what took me down the path that brought me to where I am today.

CHAPTER FOUR

A NEW DREAM

There are threads that run through our lives, connecting the different parts in ways we sometimes don't even see. In my life, it was hunger that wove through every part, and continued to drive me forward. Not only the constant hunger for food, but a hunger for opportunity.

While I was playing street soccer on Apollon's team, my teammate Louisino, let me in on something he knew about a local organized club team called Valencia.

"Valencia is feeding people," Louisino told me quietly, so that the other kids around us couldn't hear.

He did not want to simply give away the secret of where to get food. If everyone heard, they would all try out for Valencia and raise the competition to get on the team, and to get fed.

The opportunity was tempting, but I wasn't sure.

I COULD KICK A BALLOON
AROUND IN A DIRTY STREET,
BUT I CERTAINLY WASN'T
READY TO PLAY FOR A REAL
SOCCER TEAM.

But Louisino thought I could make it with the Valencia youth team.

"You should go," he whispered, more insistent. "They're feeding people."

To be honest, I was afraid to play for a real soccer team, but the draw of getting a free meal while playing a game I enjoyed was too much to turn down.

NOT GOOD ENOUGH

I had been playing barefoot, and that was my plan for Valencia.

I had sandals, but I could not wear those while playing soccer. In fact, when I played soccer, I would actually "wear" my sandals on my hands. I learned quickly that leaving my sandals at the side of the playing field meant they would disappear during the match. Even today, if you go to Haiti, you'll see kids playing soccer with sandals on their hands.

Having sandals was a big deal. If you had sandals, it meant your parents had money that month. If you lost them or someone took them, you might not have any to wear for five or six months, until the next time your parents had extra money. Shoes were not a necessity in Haiti; you could walk barefoot if you had to. But if you had sandals, you'd better hang on to them.

I also had my tennis shoes that I would wear on Sundays. My Sunday shoes were new to me, but were actually secondhand shoes. They were the kind of sports shoes someone in America might use to mow the lawn or donate to a charity after they were worn out. In fact, most of the clothes in Haiti come from America through charitable organizations that collect donations they cannot sell.

Still, those were my good Sunday shoes. They had an important role to play each week.

In Haiti, we have a tradition where we would walk around to different houses on Sundays, often the homes of the elders, wearing our best clothes and shoes. We'd give hugs while visiting, and ask if they could give us any food. They would feed us something if they had food in the house. Sunday was God's day, so people would do most of their cooking on that day, and there was usually good food to eat.

Sunday best, with your Sunday shoes, meant you could get a free meal.

But shoes were important for soccer too, and so I decided to wear my Sunday shoes. It just was not acceptable to play organized soccer barefoot.

At my first practice with Valencia, it was clear that Louisino had oversold my skills to the coach to get me on the team.

I know why he did that. He wanted to make sure that I'd get a plate of food. And I probably looked the part of a great soccer player because I was tall. There's a danger of overselling something though. You look even worse when you can't live up to the hype.

At the first practice, I was terrified. My heart was beating loud enough that I thought the coach would know the truth—that I wasn't a great player at all. I didn't want to practice. I just wanted to get something to eat. I couldn't wait for practice to be over so I could get my food and leave.

We had to run a few laps around the field, and I thought I would die. I'm sure the other players were having the same struggle I was, fighting hunger and thirst in the intense sun and heat. After practice was over, I got my plate of beans and rice. I had a little bit of water left in the small plastic bag that each of us had been given at the start of practice.

It was tough, but I decided to come back to the next practice. I wanted to keep being fed, and no one had told me yet that I wasn't good enough to come back.

In the following weeks, my playing time during practice became less and less. The few minutes I was on the field, I played horribly. I slid around in my Sunday shoes and fell over.

Finally, in February, after just a few months, the coach broke the news to me.

"We're getting closer to competition," he said, explaining that I wasn't good enough to play in the real matches. "You can still come to practice, but we're not going to feed you."

I continued going to practice each day, even without the promise of food, but it wasn't long before I was told I wasn't good enough and I should not come back.

I was surprised at how disappointed that made me. As much as soccer had become part of my life in a roundabout way, I'd actually grown to like it. Street soccer had been fun, and it hurt hearing the Valencia youth coach tell me I wasn't good enough. I was embarrassed and angry, and it took some of the joy out of the game.

But back to street soccer I went, playing in tournaments, kicking around the balloon ball. I assumed this was the furthest soccer would ever take me.

DEFEATING THE PAST

Cavaly was the rival team to Valencia in our town. I hadn't given other organized soccer teams much thought, especially since

I was told I wasn't good enough. It turns out the coach from the Cavaly youth team, Gabriel Augusmat, saw me playing in a street tournament. He liked what he saw, and invited me to play for his team. Augusmat's nickname was Zagallo, after Mario Zagallo, one of the most successful Brazilian soccer players and coaches of all time.

Fortunately, playing with Cavaly was far different than my experience with Valencia. With Cavaly, I made the youth team's lineup and even though they didn't feed the players after practice, I started enjoying soccer again. After I made the team, my parents finally found out I had been playing organized soccer. Augusmat had to ask my parents permission for me to travel to other cities to play with Cavaly. They consented, but my mother was not happy I had been playing soccer without telling her. She believed that putting your hopes on soccer would not take you anywhere in Haiti. A good education was the most important thing.

But with Cavaly, I was finally getting a taste of soccer success. In fact, the first three goals I ever scored were during the first match of the "Operation 2006" Local Counties Tournament[1] for Cavaly—a match we won 6–1.

Cavaly continued winning, and we ended up playing in the local club tournament's finals against Valencia, and it was an intense game. The rivalry between Cavaly and Valencia is one of the most well-known soccer rivalries in all of Haiti. It matters to everyone, young and old. Some fans even pledge to NEVER wear the color of the opposing team, saying they would choose death if forced to wear the other team's color. The rivalry between the fans even turned violent sometimes.

---

1. *Operation 2006* was the name for the Haitian National Team's 2006 World Cup preparation program, running from 1998 to 2006.

The day of the finals, people turned out in massive crowds to see what would happen. They were there to watch me. The story of how Valencia had rejected me before Cavaly took me on had spread, and everyone likes an underdog story.

In the first three minutes I missed a shot over the goal, and the Valencia crowd heckled and booed me. But two minutes later I had another chance. I made the same run and my teammate passed a long ball over the top. I outpaced the defenders and controlled the ball, and then I was one-on-one with the goalkeeper. This time, I faked the shot, the goalkeeper dove for it, and I dribbled right past him into the empty net. The Valencia fans were silent as Cavaly's fans erupted in cheers. That day we defeated Valencia 3–0, and I scored all three goals.

When the final whistle blew, fans climbed over the fence and ran on the field towards me. They were all wearing red, our color, so I knew I was safe. They gathered around me and started throwing me in the air. I remembered the street tournament when we had beat the rival team, and thought that this must be what Louisino had felt that day, getting cheered and tossed in the air. It all felt like I was living in a dream.

That match was a real triumph for me. It felt as if I'd defeated something from my past that had been haunting me.

After that, soccer started to become my dream. I had already been enjoying it, but I never really saw myself as a great player. Watching World Cup soccer was almost a national holiday in Haiti, and I remember thinking as I watched the players on TV, that their skill almost seemed magical. I couldn't compare to that.

But I'd had a taste of it.

Unfortunately, my mother still wasn't sold on soccer. She wanted me to concentrate on my schooling. She also worried about me getting injured, and not having enough money to pay for medical services.

I was determined though. I had helped defeat the team that had rejected me.

> *I WAS WILLING TO PUT IN THE HARD WORK TO SEE WHERE SOCCER COULD TAKE ME.*

SOMETHING BETTER

In July of 1998, I was selected for Léogâne's City team because I'd scored eleven goals in five games while playing with Cavaly. In less than six months I went from a club team to the city team, which was a selection of the eighteen best youth players in all of Léogâne.

There was a regional tournament in the nearby town of Petit-Goave *[Pè-ti-Gwav]*, and the first match we played was another victory. However, my team's success in the first game against Carrefour *[Kar-four]*, didn't sit well with some. They tried to claim that we were cheating, and that because I was so tall and muscular, I must be older than I'd said I was. Most of the Carrefour team, though very good, were physically small. Our size was partly why we won, and if the accusation about my age was proven true, I would be removed from the league and the victory would be forfeit.

"We won't let him play unless we see his birth certificate from the county records," was the official decision. My coaches,

Zagallo and Daniel Mentor, had a copy of my birth certificate, but the tournament officials wouldn't accept that version. They wanted confirmation of my age from the county.

Our next match in that tournament was the following day, Sunday. The county records, which would be needed to verify my age, were at the courthouse in Léogâne, which was over an hour away by car and was closed on weekends.

Even though this was youth soccer, they were making a big deal out of the situation. They were insistent that if my age couldn't be proven, I couldn't play on Sunday. I would be able to play on Monday if all the paperwork came through after the courthouse reopened and verified my age. But in a tournament, every match is important. Playing on Monday wouldn't help us advance in the tournament if we lost on Sunday.

Daniel Mentor, who was my assistant coach at Cavaly and the coach of my current tournament team, stepped up to help. He was a star of the Cavaly professional team and I had been watching him play on Sundays for as long as I could remember—in most cases from the top of a building or a tall tree branch. When I was younger, Daniel had held my hand to help me get inside the stadium after matches to see the other players. Not only was he a star of the team, he was a leader that everyone in my town looked up to.

Daniel remembered that I attended a Catholic primary school, the same school he had attended, and that our school was known for keeping excellent records. He called one of the teachers at my school, who was also a big soccer fan, to see if he could help prove my age.

Fortunately, the records they found at the school were accepted by the league, and I was able to play in our match on Sunday. At that point, we were ready to fight. Soccer was everything, and after the accusations of cheating, we had something to prove. I scored four goals in that match, and we won.

Our victory streak continued and, in the finals, we beat the tournament host team, Petit-Goave—a team with fans known to throw rocks and start fights if they lose. I scored the two goals that led us to victory. Sure enough, they began throwing rocks and calling me names, pressing against the rope boundary around the field.

I didn't care. I felt untouchable.

When that tournament was over, I was the top scorer.

I'd gone from kicking a tennis ball in front of my mother's restaurant, through dirty streets and the humiliation of rejection, to being the top scorer in a regional tournament in just one year.

God had given me a talent that people did not always recognize; even I hadn't realized it. My faith was still new to me, and the seeds had been planted only recently, but I began seeing God working in my life. He was showing me a new opportunity. I had to work hard and invest in it, but it was paying off. School was still very important to me, and I was just a young teenager, but I was starting to understand how soccer could be a vehicle to lead me toward a better life.

I had started playing on a team just to get free meals, but now, soccer was becoming something much bigger.

CHAPTER FIVE

FOLLOWING OPPORTUNITY

The competitive nature of life in Haiti meant that one win, one accomplishment, was never the end. It was just one rung of the ladder. There was always another level above you. You always had to compete to stay alive.

Playing with Cavaly in regional tournaments had given me the opportunity to show my skills, and I was chosen to compete in the tournament where they would choose the Haitian Youth National Team. If I played well enough there, I would have the chance to be on the Operation 2006 Youth National Team, which was named that way because the team's goal was to make it to the 2006 World Cup in Germany.

But there was an enormous obstacle, and it was my mother.

Making the youth national team had many benefits. There would be travel, food, free schooling, and the chance at a soccer career. It seemed like this would be easy to sell to my mother. But as soccer became a bigger part of my life, little by little, school became less important. My mother still believed a good education was the only chance I had for a better life. She didn't think I was good enough to have a successful soccer career. And on top of that, she was afraid I would get injured, and left with no future.

My father was a different story. He was a tough man, and he knew from his own life that without an education, it wasn't easy. Yet he could see how much I wanted to do this. He was also getting feedback from others in town about my soccer skills.

"Your son is doing good!" people would tell him. "Keep him going in soccer!"

That made him proud of me, and he started to believe.

My parents did not agree on what I should do, and it became a sore spot between them. My mother supported continuing my secondary school education at Lycée Anacaona de Léogâne. My father supported continuing my soccer career.

"He'll get to travel," my father said. "He will get to eat three times a day. Can you feed him three times a day?"

We had only a week to decide, and my parents fought about it until the day I would have to make a choice. We were all stressed, and I didn't know who would have the last word.

FINALLY, MY FATHER TOLD ME TO GO AND BE WHAT I COULD BE.

He, like many other parents in Haiti, hoped to gain some worth through their children. So at age thirteen, I traveled to Port-au-Prince to try for the Haitian Youth National Team.

MY BIG BREAK

After a long, hot bus ride from Léogâne, my team pulled up to the National Center.

I was anxious to see what the other players, the fields, and the Center looked like. My heart was beating fast with nervous energy, but as I got off the bus I acted as tough as I could. I wanted everyone to see me as a strong soccer player. There were teams from all over the country, each filled with kids my age trying for the same thing.

The National Center was like something from television. Everything was clean and new looking. I wanted nothing more than to make the Youth National Team and live there. I would play my heart out for this opportunity.

That first night, even though the bed was the most comfortable thing I had ever laid in, I didn't sleep at all. I was so anxious to get on the field and seize this opportunity.

The competition for the youth national team was fierce. Every player knew exactly how much was on the line, and no one was giving up easily. In one of the first matches against Cap-Haïtien, I scored two goals and my team won 3–1. Despite my nerves, I had played well and was hopeful about my chances.

In the next match against St. Marc, I scored three goals in the first half alone, but in the second half, my worst nightmare came true. At one point I did a bicycle kick, sending the ball into the top corner of the net. I landed on my wrist and immediately felt a searing pain. When I looked down, I could see the bone jutting out of my skin.

I raised my broken right hand, and the first thing I said was, "I can't go to school anymore!"

I started to cry. I hadn't even started my soccer career, and it looked like it was already over. My mother's fears were coming true. I'd thrown away my spot in a good school. I wouldn't be selected for the youth national team, and I'd get stuck in a low-quality private school. And even worse, I'd been injured in the process.

I passed out from the pain of it all.

Getting hurt in Haiti can be the end of a dream. The healthcare services are lacking, especially if you don't have much money. There was a good chance an injury like mine would not get fixed correctly. Sometimes broken legs would be treated by boiling corn, putting it on the leg, and then wrapping it in a bandage. There are many stories of players getting injured, and having their soccer careers end because there were few medical options to turn to.

At the hospital, I mostly remember being in pain, physically and emotionally. It was a bad break, but luckily the doctors set my wrist in a cast.

After the doctors had tended to me, I met Daniel Pierre-Charles, the Director of the Ministry of Sport for Haiti, who was very involved in the national team selection. He had waited with me at the hospital because I was there alone. He saw how upset I was over the injury, as my dream seemingly fell apart in front of me.

"Ricardo, you don't need to worry," he told me with his heavy Mexican-Haitian accent. "You're the first of twenty-five players selected for the Operation 2006 Youth National Team."

I was shocked and I didn't know what to say. I thought maybe I was still unconscious from the injury, and I was imagining him saying this to me. My injury had taken me out of the tournament, and I assumed my dreams were dead. I had been incredibly depressed and discouraged, and yet, I was now being told my dream was alive and well.

It was a very overwhelming experience. I remember sitting with my teammates the night after I broke my wrist, after I returned from the hospital. I was crying so much, and they all felt sorry for me, thinking I was in so much pain. It was true—I was in pain, but I was also overcome with the miracle God was working in my life. There was every reason for me not to make that team, but those seeds of my faith kept growing, and I could feel God's presence. I knew he had a plan for me.

Suddenly, I found myself the center of media attention. "Ricardo Pierre-Louis, first player chosen for the team!" headlines read. The attention came with plenty of controversy, however. People talked about how I didn't really prove myself since I was injured so early.

And let's not forget the competitive aspect. There was no limit to the number of kids in Haiti who were good at soccer. Playing for the national team was the dream of so many, and they'd worked just as hard as I had. The regular process for selection started with fifty kids, chosen from the selection tournament. Then they would have to demonstrate their technical skills and go through an interview process. From that, only twenty-five were chosen.

I didn't have to go through any of that.

It seemed unfair that I was given a spot without even finishing the tournament and skipping the whole process, and people made it known. But the decision-makers saw something in me. In just the first few matches I played, I had scored five goals against the best teams. And without me, my team lost in the semifinals of the tournament.

That counted for something. And I was officially on the Haitian Youth National Team.

A DIFFERENT WORLD

I remember the day I got home from the tournament. I knew my life was about to change, but my parents didn't know anything that had happened.

I walked up to the house with my broken wrist, and my mother put her hands on her head and started to cry and yell. All she saw was that my right arm was in a cast, which meant there would be no more school.

She was angry with me. She was angry with my father. She didn't want to hear what I had to say.

A man on our street saw what was happening and ran over to the house to break the news to my mother. "It's okay," he told her excitedly. "He was chosen for the national team!"

The news was some comfort to her, but remember, school and education were everything to my mother. She accepted that I wanted to play soccer, but she wasn't happy about the prospect of me leaving the school we had competed so hard for. She also knew that playing for the youth national team meant I would move to the National Center to live.

My mother struggled with this because visits would be rare. But my father again pushed for me to seize the opportunity.

He saw it as an investment. You could keep your money in a savings account and it would stay safe. Or you could take a chance by putting it in the stock market and see what would happen. My mother wanted to keep me on a safe, known path, but my father saw that the opportunity was there. Who knew where it would lead?

Soccer had become my dream, and I didn't want to let this opportunity pass. So, one week later with my arm still in a cast, off to the National Center I went.

Everything I owned fit into a single bag.

My parents came along with me for orientation day. My mother was nervous, knowing that she would meet important people and wanting to make a good impression. She wore her best clothes and was careful about her manners. My father, on the other hand, was so excited by everything he saw and the opportunity I was going to have.

The National Center is well-funded, and they were preparing us for the World Cup. We had three meals a day. We each had personal psychologists in case there were conflicts between players. There were staff who would wash our clothes and clean our rooms. There were people who came on the weekends to arrange for social activities, which helped keep us out of trouble.

I think seeing all of this helped my mother accept what I was doing, and the path I was on. She saw that I would have good living conditions and people watching out for me.

As orientation day came to an end, my parents had to leave, and I was finally on my own.

My first impression of my room was that it was extremely clean. It looked brand new compared to anything I had ever seen. I had several roommates—some of whom remain my friends to this day—and each of us was experiencing something completely new. This overwhelming experience, and the fact that we were all teenage boys, led to several of our disagreements.

One of my roommates, Stephane, was a tall, skinny boy from St. Marc in the central-western part of Haiti. My other roommate, Johnson, was a small boy from Port-de-Paix *[Pòr-de-Pè]* in the northwest. On one particular night, a couple weeks after we had moved to the Center, Stephane wanted to turn the light off and go to bed, but Johnson wasn't tired. I could not get them to compromise, so I let them continue arguing.

Pretty soon Johnson was attacking Stephane in the middle of our room. Stephane, being much bigger than Johnson, grabbed his arm and smacked him in the face a couple times. In Haiti, we don't want to break up a fight too soon because we like to get a good laugh out of it first. Johnson grabbed the broom from the hallway, but Stephane easily got it out of his hands. Eventually, Johnson accepted his loss and went to bed. But the fight was not over. The next morning, while Stephane and I were sleeping, Johnson sneaked over to Stephane's bed with the broom in hand.

Right before he made his move, I woke up and screamed, "Johnson, don't you dare!" Stephane finally woke up but instead of being angry, he started laughing. Then we were all laughing. We went around and told all the other players the story, with Stephane and Johnson laughing about it the whole time. It was one of my favorite days at the Center—a day of truly feeling like a kid having fun with his friends.

Meeting kids from all over Haiti was an eye-opening experience. I was never familiar with how people lived in other parts of the country, or even how some of them spoke with different accents. It was like a North Dakotan meeting a Tennessean for the first time. We would laugh all day at how each other's voices sounded.

For the first time in my life, I was able to be a kid. Most of my childhood had been so focused on school that there hadn't been room for anything else. At the Center, I was around my friends all the time, playing soccer and living with them. My childhood had also been concentrated around hunger; wondering where my next meal would come from. At the Center, I never had to worry about meals. We were fed three times a day, every day, without fail.

It was a different world.

A day at the Center meant early morning soccer training, followed by a full day of classes at the school near the Center, with training again after school. In my first two weeks living there I had to sit out of soccer practice because of my injured wrist. I was eager to start practicing, and luckily everything had healed well and I was able to play as soon as the cast came off.

On weekends, we would sometimes train in the morning, and then spend the day doing social or civic activities. Learning how to be a leader was another important part of being at the Center.

In our little free time, we would watch a lot of soccer on television.

> EVERYTHING WAS SOCCER AT THE CENTER, AND SOCCER WAS THE RELIGION THERE.

We did not go to church on Sundays. Instead, we watched professional matches from the European leagues in the morning. Each of us was also connected to our city teams and we would listen to the Haitian Professional League soccer matches on the radio. At night, before we went to bed, we would watch or listen to the sports report.

Since soccer took the place of religion at the Center, my faith didn't have much of a chance to grow. I did not have a Bible, and I was afraid to be seen as the weird one. No one there read the Bible. It was simply not part of the culture. While I was there, I sometimes imagined that if I did have a Bible, I would try to be like Jesus. I thought I would sneak away from everyone at night, or early in the morning, to read the scripture and spend time with God. I never ceased praying to God, but my faith could not flourish. I was a brand new Christian, and the seeds of my faith were having trouble growing without any real guidance. It was hard, but I tried to distract myself with soccer to avoid feeling guilty about not seeking Jesus.

At the school we attended, those of us who lived at the Center received a lot of respect. We were the privileged ones. The other students watched us eat the lunches we'd packed at the center—lunches like ham sandwiches with lettuce, tomato, and Tabasco sauce, things I'd never eaten before in my life.

Passing school exams was a requirement for staying on the national team. Some players struggled, including one of my friends who failed and was kicked out of the Center. Thankfully, this school was not as challenging as my previous school in Léogâne, and I passed with ease. My mother, in her own way, contributed to my success in soccer with her insistence that I receive the best possible education.

Everything about the Center felt like a radical change moving my life towards the opportunities I was seeking. I felt a real sense of accomplishment, and I was so grateful to be there.

RICAR-GOAL!

Our first soccer match as the Youth National Team sold out.

It had been advertised as a chance to see Haiti's next World Cup team. The last time Haiti had competed in the World Cup was in 1974, so the stadium was packed.

Here we were, little thirteen-year-old kids, playing in front of twenty thousand people.

I remember that first match so clearly. It was the first time we wore our Haitian jerseys, and they were so big that the sleeves came down to our elbows. The stadium was completely red and blue. People were chanting and dancing. The roar of the crowd was deafening, and as a team, we gave them good reason to make noise. Our team destroyed the Dominican Republic, winning 9–1. I picked up a new nickname after that: *Ricar-goal.*

Soon we were getting interviewed and featured in the media. I was voted team captain, and my picture was even on the back of buses in Haiti.

I could hardly believe it. I was living the dream.

Everything was new and exciting. I was flying on airplanes, traveling, playing soccer, and getting national attention. I was so thankful to God for the miracle he made in my life. I had believed all my dreams were over when I broke my wrist, but God was there to light my way forward. I could never have imagined, just a few years earlier, how different my life would look.

When I showed my mother photos from the places I had travelled, and told her all the things I had experienced, she started to believe in me at last. She could see the good things that were happening in my life, and that I really was a great soccer player

Maybe, just maybe, my father and I had been right—there was a future for me in soccer.

DEVASTATING LOSSES

My soccer career continued to be successful through my years at the National Center, and as I got older, my next focus was competing in the Youth World Cup qualifying tournament.

When I was just about to turn seventeen, I was selected to play on the Under-17 National Team (U-17), which is the next level after the Youth National Team. If you make it to the Youth World Cup—which is a possibility when playing in U-17—you're almost guaranteed to play professionally, which was my goal. I would soon age out of living at the Center, and the only next step I could see was a professional soccer career.

While on the U-17 National Team, I was able to travel to Mexico, Brazil, and different countries in Central America. Just a few years earlier, I had never even seen an airplane, and couldn't have imagined the opportunity to fly to all these places.

My team made it to the Youth World Cup qualifying tournament in Tegucigalpa, Honduras. In our first match, we played Honduras, the tournament hosts. They were the number one seed and favored to win the whole tournament. There were more than thirty thousand people in the stadium, mostly fans of the home team, and the noise was intense. Even with all that against us, we defeated Honduras 2–0.

Despite the win, it wasn't all good news. I got two yellow cards in the match, one for trying to take time off the clock at the end, and another for a silly foul on another player. One yellow card doesn't get you kicked out of the match, but two yellow cards—which then equal a more serious red card—does.

To get into the World Cup, our team needed to defeat Mexico in our next game. Because of the red card, I wasn't allowed to play in that match. Still, we'd defeated the favored home team in the World Cup tournament, so we weren't terribly worried during our first victory celebration.

Before our next match with Mexico, reality set in. I was a key player, and without me our team played the worst it had in the past two years. We lost 7–1. It was a tough loss, but we still had a chance to make the Youth World Cup. The dream hadn't died yet. We had to beat Costa Rica in our next match and I would get to play in that game.

In the eighty-seventh minute of play against Costa Rica, they scored. We had three minutes left, but all our attempts to score failed. We lost 1–0. It was an extremely devastating loss. We watched as Mexico went on to play in the Youth World Cup, while we returned to Haiti.

Even though I hadn't made the Youth World Cup, my soccer ability had caught the attention of other teams. Bernard Souillez, who had worked with the French National Team, was helping train coaches in Haiti at the time. He saw my talent and helped me find a contract to play for a team in Metz, France.

I went to France to try out, and made the academy team in Metz at seventeen years old. They signed me on a future-pro contract, which meant I would play with the Metz Youth Academy for six months and hoped to sign onto a professional contract when I turned eighteen. I was incredibly excited for my chance to be a professional soccer player in France.

Living in France as a teenager was an exciting time for me. I had always hoped soccer would give me opportunities outside of Haiti, and it finally had! I felt like I was on the path towards everything I had ever dreamed of. I played well while I was at the Youth Academy and was looking forward to signing my first professional contract with Football Club de Metz (FC Metz). Signing professional contracts happens around Christmas. In the world of FIFA-governed soccer teams, January is when the "market" is closed and players are announced. Everything was set for me to sign the contract in December, but then things started to go wrong.

There was a rule change at the national level in France right before I was set to sign. The new rule stated that there was a limit on roster spots for international players. One of the main reasons they did this was because so many teenagers came to France from Africa and other countries to play soccer, and if they couldn't make a team, they ended up on the streets. This change overruled the future-pro contract I'd signed at the start, because now, FC Metz could only select the top eight international players in my class at the academy.

Unfortunately, I was not in the top eight at the time and I had no agent to negotiate on my behalf. I was not offered a professional contract. Instead, now-famous soccer star Emmanuel Adebayor, who had been in my class, was signed.

I had been living the dream, thinking I was on my way to making it big as an international soccer star in France. I had been imagining how I'd thank my parents for all they'd done as I climbed the ladder of success.

But that was all gone. My dream had come crashing down in a matter of days.

Feeling like a failure, I left France and returned to Haiti, unsure of what my future would be.

CHAPTER SIX

MORE THAN A GAME

When I was ten years old, I had climbed a tree that overlooked the soccer stadium in my hometown of Léogâne so I could watch a match. The stadium was packed that day. Cavaly was going up against Violettes, which meant two of the Haitian National Team stars going head-to-head. Carlo Marcelin of Cavaly was known as the playmaker, and was a mastermind on the soccer field. Wilfrid Montilas of Violettes was a larger-than-life figure. He was a tough player, and an extremely skilled defender. That day, Cavaly defeated Violettes 2–1 by a late goal.

I'll never forget that match because as soon as it was over, I rushed down the tree and climbed the stadium wall, sneaking through the fans surrounding Montilas. I felt like Zaccheus hurrying down the tree and through the crowds to meet Jesus. Eventually, I stood right in front of Montilas. He was massive, with veins all over his legs and arms. To me, he looked like a giant monster with his fierce competitive face. His eyes were bloodshot from tears after losing the match, which gave him an even more out-of-this-world quality. He didn't seem real to me.

At ten years old, soccer was already more than a game; those players were gods to me. Back then, I didn't think I could ever be one, and yet, in my teenage years, I had come so close. My chance at becoming a professional player in France had given me hope that I could have a real career in soccer. But when that chance came crashing down, I felt like that ten-year-old again, climbing a tree just to get a glimpse of the soccer gods— on the outside, looking in.

DESPITE MY DISAPPOINTMENT, IT SEEMED GOD HAD STILL PLANNED A PATH FORWARD FOR ME.

THE GOLD CUP

In early 2002, two months after I returned to Haiti from France, I was called to try out for the full Haitian National Team. The team was preparing for the CONCACAF Gold Cup in Miami and was led by the famous Argentinian coach Jorge Castelli. Even though it was an honor to be selected, I was the youngest player trying out for the national team at seventeen, and believed I had no chance to make the twenty-five-man roster. Among the fifty players selected to try out were some of the most famous Haitian soccer players ever, including Golman Pierre, Jean-Robert Menelas, Gabriel Michel (Tigana), Wilfrid Montilas, Frantz Gilles, Jean-Muller Altidor, Pierre-Richard Bruny, Peter Germain, and many more.

Walking into that first practice for the National Team, I felt like that ten-year-old standing in front of Wilfrid Montilas all over again. Being on the same field as these players, but this time as a teammate, was something I had never imagined when I was growing up. I was looking into the faces of players I had admired my whole life. I desperately wanted to show them I deserved to be there and to redeem my failure in France.

As practices continued, famous players were getting cut daily, but I was still there. Two days before the final roster of twenty-five was to be announced, I was in my top form. I knew I had two choices: fail, go back to Léogâne, and live with regrets; *or* make the team, show everyone how good I was, have another shot at signing a professional contract, and make my family proud. I didn't want to go back home with nothing, and a fire was lit inside me to prove I was good enough for the national team.

When the roster was announced, I was listed as one of the top twenty-five players. That year, the famous Haitian National Team beat the renowned Álex Aguinaga and Ecuador in the quarterfinals of the Gold Cup in Miami, and I got to be there for it.

Nothing could describe the emotions of that Gold Cup match. I was only seventeen and hadn't experienced anything like it before. We beat a team that was ranked in the top ten FIFA standings.

I remember the bus ride back from the Orange Bowl stadium in Miami. Wilfrid Montilas was chanting the whole way, calling himself "Men Lalas," or in English "the real deal." I could not stop asking myself if this was all just a dream. My teammates were soccer gods in Haiti. I remember thinking that if I died tomorrow, I would die a happy man.

One might say soccer is just a game, but that is not the truth.

You have to understand what soccer means in Haiti, especially for poor Haitians like my family. The struggles my parents endured were passed on to me. There was so little chance of me escaping that cycle of poverty. The odds of me being a part of that Gold Cup team were too slim to even imagine. God had truly blessed my life for this to happen.

After the Gold Cup tournament, I was chosen to be on the Under-20 National Team (U-20) as I was still only eighteen years old. This meant I had to be a part of a local club team, so that I was an active player when the national team called me up to play with them.

I was playing with Cavaly again, but there was a major problem for my future as a professional soccer player: I wasn't getting any playing time.

THE IMPORTANCE OF SHOES

Even after playing with the National Team and nearly becoming a professional player in France, I was sitting on the bench back in Léogâne with Cavaly. There was some tension in Léogâne over the situation. Some thought I should be playing, but others felt that the current Cavaly players shouldn't be benched—especially if they hadn't played poorly—just because I had joined the team again. The coach could get in trouble or even fired if he pulled a fan-favorite top scorer, like Daniel Mentor or Jackson Dalce, who had been playing with Cavaly for years, just so I could play.

Throughout that time with Cavaly, I was desperately hoping for another chance to play professionally, and a few times I came close, but nothing ever worked out. Life became hard and emotional for me. At eighteen, I was feeling depressed about my future as a soccer player, and my future in general. Everyone saw me as this big star because of the opportunities I'd had, but inside, I was really struggling. I was angry that things were not working out, and I even stepped away from my faith in God, which had always been my biggest source of strength throughout my journey.

I was getting hopeless and frustrated with sitting on the bench. I knew I was good enough to play, but it seemed there was nothing I could do because of the politics of the team. But one day, a teammate and childhood hero of mine changed all that.

It was halftime of an important match. The game was tied 0–0 and I was sitting on the bench as usual, but could tell something was a little different that day. During halftime, my team was waiting in the locker room when Daniel Mentor— the man who had been my coach years earlier, and a player I had watched from that tree by the stadium when I was ten— walked up to our coach and told him I should be playing.

He said even if I had to take his spot, I should have the opportunity. Then he did something incredible. He bent down, unlaced his cleats, and took them off in front of the coach.

The locker room was silent.

In Haiti, speaking up against something that is corrupt is almost unheard of. Everyone is afraid of retaliation or losing opportunities. In Haitian soccer, the coach is always right, no matter what. Despite any influence or corruption from outside forces, players don't question the coach. There is no speaking up, no suggestions on how to do things differently, even if there are five other guys who can do a better job out on the field.

For Mentor to stand up for me, in front of the coach, was something I had never seen before. His career was on the line, but he wanted to see action that day instead of just words. He was the star of Cavaly, and he used the power that had won over the city, the fans, and the coach to advocate on my behalf. He believed that I should be playing if I was good enough, and that nothing should get in the way. Not my age, not the fans, and not even the team management.

I will never forget his courage in that moment.

Everyone was astonished. When I walked onto the field after halftime, the crowd was shocked. They were stunned into silence, and I could tell that if I failed, that same crowd would explode. It was an important match for Cavaly's standing in the league, and I was replacing one of the best players on the team. I knew I couldn't waste this chance to finally play, and I didn't. During that second half, I was able to assist on a goal, and we won 1–0 that day.

In over forty years of Cavaly history, I was probably the only eighteen-year-old who made it into the lineup. Mentor changed the unwritten rules for me. What he did was extremely significant, and some of my teammates called me the luckiest soccer player alive. It was God's vision, though, not luck. I recalled my first time trying to play city soccer without any shoes. Now Daniel had removed his own shoes in deference to me.

I FELT THE GRAVITY OF THE MOMENT LIKE IT WAS A SEED RISING UP OUT OF THE DIRT, GROWING FROM POVERTY AND INSIGNIFICANCE.

To this day, I keep in contact with Mentor. That moment had such a huge impact on me, and changed the direction of my life from then on. His gesture meant way more to me than just getting more playing time. I was in awe of his display of integrity, and his faith in me and my abilities.

I played in every match for Cavaly after that. It seemed as if a new dream was possible. I was feeling more hopeful about what was in front of me. Though the path had been winding, I could see that a future in soccer was still a possibility.

SAVING A LIFE

We were playing a match against Racing des Gonaives, a team that is well-known in Haiti for having won many league titles, when something happened that demonstrated so clearly the power that soccer players have in Haiti.

The match started off well. At one point during a corner kick, I made a double move right, then left, and jumped five feet in the air to head the ball across to the front post. The goalkeeper made a spectacular save on my header, probably the best save of his career. Our fans sensed we were close to scoring and were cheering and dropping red smoke bombs onto the field.

It was about the seventy-fifth minute where things became a bit more interesting.

I was in the box, about to take a shot, and I did my lightspeed double step-over. The defender veered right and I went left, a bit off-balance. He tackled me and I dove into the box with no resistance. The referee should have called a penalty on that play and given me a penalty kick, but he didn't.

A few minutes later, right before the match ended, the referee called a silly penalty, causing us to lose. The fans went wild with anger.

I could see people climbing the fences around the stadium, breaking onto the field. A large crowd was rushing toward the referee, looking like they might not let him leave peacefully.

Our team was ushered down to the locker room to shower. It was getting dark at that point, and since our stadiums did not have lights, we couldn't see how serious the situation was getting on the field.

After showering, we were all about to leave when someone from the United Nations came to us.

The UN was in Haiti at the time due to some political issues. They were there to bring peace to the nation, but we certainly didn't expect them to call on us right in our own stadium.

"You guys, you have to help. It's getting dark, and no one can see a thing," the UN official said. We weren't sure what he was talking about. "You need to put your uniforms back on."

Our uniforms were dirty. We'd showered. We had plans after the match. We couldn't understand why we would need to put our uniforms back on and return to the darkening field. Was there some kind of penalty kick they wanted us to do? It didn't make sense.

The UN official was insistent, even as we tried to dismiss the request. Three of our best players relented, myself included. We put our jerseys back on.

When we got to the field, people were angry and fighting. They were so upset about that final call by the referee, who was now trapped on the field in a circle of enraged fans. They were throwing things at him, hitting him, and refusing to let him leave. The UN had tried to evacuate the stadium by driving their tanks on the field to scare the crowd into dispersing, but they wouldn't budge. The fans fought right back, throwing rocks in all directions; they did not care if they were arrested or if they died—Cavaly was their life.

The fans screamed to the UN soldiers that the referee wasn't going anywhere. He was going to sleep there, maybe even die there.

We were nervous when we realized what was going on. With an angry crowd like that, we could easily get hurt ourselves.

"You're the only ones who can get that referee out," the UN official said.

He wasn't wrong. We couldn't leave that referee out there.

So we went, pushing our way through the angry mob of people. We found the referee in the middle of the crowd, crying and shaking. We grabbed his hand and walked him out, trying to get back to the locker room. The crowd followed us the whole way, attempting to hit the referee until we made it to safety. I had to push some people back to prevent him from getting really hurt.

I could hear the angry shouts in heavy Creole, "Jezi sove w jodia, ou met kontinye priye."

They were telling him, "Jesus saved you. You would have been dead. You need to keep praying to your God."

We waited in the locker room until the crowd went home. The referee was sent home in a car, escorted by the UN. That night, I was so thankful that I prayed to God for the first time in awhile. It was God's grace that helped us save the referee.

There is power in soccer, enough to appease an angry crowd, and at least for that evening, the referee must have been thankful for that power.

It may have saved his life.

A GAME OF PEACE

Things continued to go well for me, but there was always an underlying sense of fear.

Even though I was playing for Cavaly and the National Team, I was living with the constant worry of what I could lose. I knew how easily things could change and how quickly my life could go from good to struggling to survive.

In February of 2004, President Jean-Bertrand Aristide was forced to resign in a coup d'état after the rebel leader, Guy Philippe, invaded Haiti from the Dominican. Philippe had been a police chief under the Aristide regime, and claimed that Aristide had been funding and aiding the gangs in Haiti to help keep him in power. During that time, the police force could not get control of the gangs, as many had police badges, uniforms, and guns, allegedly provided to them by the government. No one could actually tell who was police and who was part of a gang.

It was a time of violence and chaos, and in June of that year, UN peacekeeping forces arrived to provide security while rule of law was reestablished. France also sent troops to protect French citizens living in Haiti.

Unfortunately, the UN and French forces added to the problem. Violent clashes with Haitians left many dead. Human rights violations, such as physical and sexual assaults, resulted in many broken lives in Haiti. Abused women and girls were left to raise children alone. Some neighborhoods were decimated by gunfire. The gangs responded by revolting against the UN and French troops, while still continuing their war against Haitian police and civilians.

Haiti was in a downward spiral of violence and death, with no end in sight. That is, until August, when I played the biggest soccer match of my life.

It was known as the Game of Peace.

The Haitian National Team played a match against Brazil, the defending World Cup champions of that year. The president of Brazil knew how powerful soccer was in Haiti, and he called for this game to give soccer a chance to do its work. As World Cup champions, Brazil would not normally come to Haiti just to play a friendly match, but the Brazilian government knew it was important, and many of the UN soldiers present in Haiti were from Brazil, and had experienced the troubling violence firsthand.

The match was meant to draw the world's attention to what was going on in Haiti. Another goal was to encourage armed factions in the country to turn over their guns — which many believed had been illegally provided by the government — and work towards peace.

This was a tense time in the nation, but also a chance to see the power of soccer play out on a bigger stage than what I'd experienced before. It became one of the matches FIFA used to show the world that soccer is more than just a game, and that the passion of soccer can help alleviate poverty and bring peace.

For me, the Game of Peace was a chance to play against the best players in the world, the players I watched on TV. In the national stadium in Port-au-Prince, the crowd size would normally be twenty thousand to thirty thousand people. But for the Game of Peace, there were fifty thousand people inside and around one million people watching outside. People had come from all over the nation for a chance to see the Brazilian team, hoping to catch a glimpse of soccer star Ronaldo as he rode by in a UN tank on his way to the stadium. This would be their only chance to ever see him in person.

The stadium was about twenty kilometers from the airport. People followed Ronaldo and the other players the whole way, sobbing and cheering, overwhelmed with it all. Tanks carried the players to keep them safe, but also so that the public could see them along the route. The noise of the crowds was like nothing I'd heard, a kind of dull roar and wail of excitement, a noise that never stopped or dimmed as the players waved from the top of the tanks, with people pressing in. There were drums and chants and people carrying both the Haitian and Brazilian flags. The excitement and emotion was incredible, like pure hope and energy all at once.

It was a memorable match for me for so many reasons. I was able to talk to Ronaldo in person, which was an incredible moment. The experience of playing in front of *that* crowd, for *that* purpose, against *that* team is something that will never be topped in my entire soccer career. We could all feel the hope radiating from the stands in that stadium.

> THE IDEA FOR THE MATCH WAS TO HAVE THE TWO TEAMS PLAY, BUT THAT PEACE WOULD BE THE ULTIMATE WINNER.

And it worked!

After that game, there was peace in Haiti. People were happy for a long time. They stopped fighting in the streets, and they weren't thinking about being hungry. They were just thinking about soccer. The victorious Brazilian World Cup team, with its famous players, had come to their country and played their team.

The Bible says "blessed are the peacemakers," and I discovered that even a game like soccer can function in the role of bringing peace, whether it's to rescue a referee or to rescue a nation.

CHAPTER SEVEN

NEW COUNTRY, NEW LIFE

The hunger for opportunity was a thread woven through my life, even in the midst of soccer success.

I had seen the power of soccer in Haiti, and I was happy with the success I achieved, but I still was not satisfied. I could not forget the feeling of being told I wasn't good enough when I first started playing at Valencia, and I wanted so badly to sign a professional contract.

I wanted to leave Haiti. I wanted more.

The Under-20 (U-20) World Cup qualifiers in Charleston, South Carolina, was my last chance to make it to the World Cup, and possibly my last chance to play professionally. As players get older, it becomes more and more difficult to make the leap to a professional league.

At the qualifiers, my Haitian team was scheduled to play against Canada, the US, and El Salvador.

Henry Moyo, a coach from Lee University, a small Christian college in Cleveland, Tennessee, happened to be at the tournament scouting. He didn't know who I was, though he did have some Haitian players on his university team who I'd played against before. Moyo had come on a whim since the qualifiers were so close to his home in Tennessee. Little did he know that the future God had planned for me rested in his hands.

I played well in our match against the US, and after the match, another Haitian playing in the tournament came up to me and said that there was a coach who wanted to speak to me.

That was the first time I met Coach Moyo.

Moyo indicated that he liked what he'd seen. "You played really well," he said. "I'd like to offer you a full scholarship to come play for me."

I looked at the other Haitian to translate. "What does he mean?"

"Have you heard of the NCAA?"

He explained to me that I would play for the university, and they would pay for my schooling.

It was something I hadn't even considered. I was focused on becoming a professional player, and this coach was asking me about playing college soccer. I wasn't sure what to do at that point, so I said I would think about it.

THE PATH TO AMERICA

Our team did not qualify for the Under-20 World Cup in that tournament. We lost to the US and tied Canada and El Salvador, but those two ties weren't enough to take us any further. I went back to Haiti, but I couldn't stop thinking about the offer from Coach Moyo. I had been waiting for an offer to play professionally, but nothing was happening. I was still playing well for Cavaly, but I had lost my spot on the national team as other strikers around the country started performing better than me.

In my hometown, the people still saw me as a soccer god. They followed me everywhere. But I had seen other acclaimed players end up begging for food in the streets. In fact, those old players would often ask me to buy them a meal. My fame made me appear happy on the outside, but deep inside, I was still hopeless and depressed. I was constantly afraid of what the future might hold—that I would fail and end up just like those players, begging the newest famous soccer star for a meal.

Halfway through the year in the summer off-season, I decided to call Coach Moyo.

"What can I do to come play for you?" I asked him, through my translator.

Coach Moyo was glad I called. He said I would need to take the SAT test if I wanted to play at Lee University.

Later that year, I asked a friend who lived in Miami about the SAT test. He explained it was a test in English, which I did not speak, and I would need my passport to take it in the United States. My friend made the arrangements, and in September of 2004, I traveled to Miami and took the test.

It wasn't nearly as easy as it might seem however. Taking the SAT was challenging because I did not speak a word of English. Up to that point, I'd never failed a major test before. In Haiti, I was always a top student in my region. But as I sat there looking at a test written in a language I couldn't understand, I knew I had very little chance of passing it. There was a moment during the test when I broke into tears because I felt like I had hit an impossible barrier to a better education and life, one I would never be able to get past.

On the reading and English portions of the test, I simply guessed. I had no clue what I was looking at. On the math portion, at least, I knew what I was doing. Math is math in any language.

I felt very discouraged after the test, knowing I had to have failed the English sections. Coach Moyo said I needed to get at least a 720 to go to Lee, and I wasn't sure that was possible. I was having my test results sent to my friend in Miami, so I waited anxiously for his call after I returned to Haiti.

A few weeks later, my friend called, excited, telling me I'd passed. But all I wanted was to know the score I got. My friend told me I scored a 530 in math, and a 200 in English. With the SAT, you get an automatic 200 points for just taking that portion of the test, so that meant I had completely failed English. And while my total score was considered "passing," I had still failed part of the test.

I called Coach Moyo as soon as I could, worried about what he'd say about my score.

"You can come with that!" he said excitedly. "But we'll put you in basic English and reading here at the university."

God had come through for me once again. I was relieved, but also wary. I wasn't sure everything would work out yet. I had no scholarship letter, no visa. I felt like I could not share this news with anyone in Haiti. I had been disappointed so many times, it was difficult to hold on to hope.

Weeks later, the letter from Lee University finally did arrive, and with that assurance, I applied for a visa.

When soccer fans found out I was leaving for America, they were not all happy about my decision.

"You are crazy for going to college in America!" they'd say to me. "You're wasting your future!"

My parents were happy with the decision, though. They were glad to see me going somewhere safe, away from the dangers of unrest in Haiti. My mother was still convinced school was the best path, and both of them were happy to be done with hearing people criticize me when I didn't play well in a match. I had been a Haitian National Team star, and I was a top scorer for Cavaly, but fans tended to have a short memory. One low-scoring match was enough to draw a lot of anger.

My mother was pleased with the idea of me being the first person in my family to graduate from college. She had persistently believed that getting an education was the most important pursuit in life. Going to Lee University was very much in line with what I had envisioned for myself as a child. I wanted to guarantee myself an opportunity for more, which is why I had worked so hard in primary school. Lee was giving me the chance to get an education and to play soccer too. While it wasn't playing soccer professionally, it was the next best thing I could imagine.

What was even better about this educational path was that I had no idea Lee was a Christian school. Not only was God answering my prayers and giving me this opportunity, but he was also directing me safely on this journey, and for His glory.

I was not a strong Christian at the time, and I made many poor decisions when it came to my faith. Still, I often prayed that God would deliver me, and he always did.

GOD HAD A MASTER PLAN, BRINGING ME TO A CHRISTIAN SCHOOL DURING THE MOST DIFFICULT TIME OF MY CAREER.

He put the right people in the right place at the right time for me.

So on January 5, 2005, I officially left Haiti to attend college in the United States. My friend in Miami, Hans, paid for my flight. Coach Moyo drove all the way from Lee University to Miami to pick me up—a nine-hour drive—because I didn't have enough money to get a flight directly to Tennessee. I stayed at the coach's house for about a week, until school started. Coach Moyo's house was a modest home by American standards, but I remember looking at his home, realizing I was going to college, and thinking, "This is the life!"

I didn't see this as giving up on a future of playing soccer professionally, but instead as choosing a road to real opportunity. I remembered when I broke my wrist in that first youth national team tournament, and how close I came to losing everything in one moment. Now I was here.

MAKING IT WORK AT LEE

My early days at Lee University were frustrating because I knew so little English. I was signed up for basic English

Reading and Writing, a special class which had other international students. But even in that class, everyone's English was better than mine. Many of them had attended a hybrid English school prior to studying in America, preparing them for university abroad.

I also took a low-level New Testament class, but understood little of what the teacher said. I found I had to use gestures or get classmates' attention to try to find out the assignments we had to do. Some were unsure what to make of me and my gestures. They didn't realize I could not understand English, and probably thought I couldn't speak or hear.

Thankfully, I was placed with three ideal suitemates, because they all helped me in their own way. One was from Nigeria, another from Jamaica, and the third from Bismarck, North Dakota, of all places. They helped me with both my English and with getting around the college. They tutored me, and helped me understand as much as possible, and thanks to them I did not get too discouraged.

In the beginning, Lee University seemed like a step backward for me in many ways. I knew I was smart; I had proved that in all my years of schooling. But trying to function in a foreign country with a foreign language made me feel slow and helpless.

I was well-known in Haiti. I had traveled around the world, been on television, and played soccer in front of tens of thousands of cheering fans. But at Lee, no one knew who I was, and most soccer games were attended by less than one hundred people. It seemed that no one there really cared about soccer, and to them, I was nobody.

During this time I really questioned God, asking if Lee University was really where He wanted me to be.

Soccer practice was a lifesaver for me. At least there I knew what I was doing, and it gave me confidence in the midst of feeling inadequate in college. Practice kept me excited for each day.

During my first few games in the spring of 2005 at Lee, I scored six goals. The opposing schools noticed my skill and began making accusations, saying that Lee University had recruited a professional soccer player. They said I was ineligible to play at the college level because I had been a professional when I played in France. Coach Moyo began thinking that maybe I had not told him the truth. It looked bad for Lee University, a Christian college, to be caught up in what seemed like a sports scandal.

I was scared, but I knew the truth. I'd never been signed to play professionally when I was in France.

Though I had desperately wanted to, I had never become a professional player. I had never received any money for playing soccer in France. But there was a demand from our competing universities that I be removed from the team and sent back to Haiti. By this time, it was almost April and I had worked hard to learn English, get settled, and fit in at Lee University. And now they were saying I would have to go back to Haiti?

I told Coach Moyo I'd never signed nor been paid to play. Anyone could look it up. They would never find any proof that I had been a professional, because there was none. Coach Moyo pushed back against the accusations, saying that what I had done at the Metz Academy in France was no different than a student attending a private school and playing soccer on their team.

The other universities conceded, and I was allowed to play, but with some conditions. One year was cut from my athletic eligibility, and I had to pass twenty-four credits by July to stay at Lee and be eligible to play in the fall. In order to earn a degree, I would have to finish college—*in English*—in three years, starting with double the required number of classes for a freshman.

I was already struggling to pass the classes I had, which only added up to twelve credits—nowhere near the twenty-four the NCAA was requiring. How was I going to get all the credits I needed in less than three months?

They were going to make sure I couldn't play, one way or another.

The athletic director didn't think I could earn the credits, and since soccer was not a priority in Lee's athletic program, he did not want to waste his time fussing over this problem. He recommended that I finish out the semester and go back to Haiti.

But if I went back to Haiti, my dream would be over. I couldn't play soccer. Even if I was good enough, someone else would have taken my spot. I'd told everyone in Haiti I wasn't going to play there anymore, that I was moving on with this new opportunity in America. I didn't know what I would do if I had to go back. Would I become a soccer beggar on the street?

But Coach Moyo had a plan, and he believed that I could pass the twenty-four credits in time. He had recruited me to the program to change it, bring it to the next level, and he wasn't going to give up easily. His job, and maybe the entire soccer program, were on the line.

"I think we can make it work," he told me.

I couldn't see how.

"You speak French, right?" he asked. I did. French was my first language.

"Do you also speak Spanish?" he asked. I had learned Spanish from some Cuban doctors at the National Center where I had lived.

I let him know I spoke Spanish as well.

"I think we can make this work, because you only need twelve more credits by July. If you test out of French I and French II, and Spanish, and then take my Old Testament class in the summer, you'll have twelve credits," he said. "But if you fail any of them, you're done."

I was already spending a lot of time studying for the classes I currently had, but I put in more time, even reviewing my Spanish and French grammar, just to be sure I would pass the exams. Thankfully, I tested out of all three language classes. I finished Coach Moyo's Old Testament class in June and had my transcripts sent to the athletic department in early July.

After all my hard work to pass those twenty-four credits, the department reviewed my records and there was no dispute with my transcript. I was eligible to play again! I remember my first match back. I was so relieved to keep my scholarship and to continue at Lee that I started crying. I scored four goals in the first twenty minutes and felt like I was walking on air.

My time at Lee University is something that I will always be grateful for. My soccer accomplishments included setting several records, including the most goals scored by any player in university history: 101. As a freshman, I was an All-American and I helped take Lee University to the NCAA Division II Nationals. I also received the honor of being inducted into Lee's athletic Hall of Fame.

While at Lee, I grew immensely in my faith. Being at a Christian university gave me the resources to fully embrace my relationship with God.

> GOD WAS ALWAYS PRESENT
> ON THE LEE CAMPUS. HIS
> PRESENCE WAS A REMINDER TO
> LEARN AND GROW EVERY DAY.

Regardless of the course of study, God was the theme of the curriculum. It was not just religion being shoved at me by students and teachers; people at Lee really cared about me and my growing faith. The culture there was all about discovering God, and loving and serving each other.

Lee University was also where I met my future wife. In my second year of school, my friend and soccer teammate, Jeff, introduced me to a woman named Nika, and she was different than anyone I'd met before. She was beautiful, smart, and kind, and I knew right away she was the one. Nika told me she was from North Dakota, just like my former suitemate, and in order to impress her, I pretended I knew where that was. As we learned more about each other, Nika and I had many deep conversations, and I remember her telling me that she wanted to change the world.

I was surprised to hear her say that. The world is a big place; how could one person change it?

Yet in some ways, Nika and I shared the same mission. As a young boy, I had tried to understand why Haiti was so poor and wondered how I could end poverty. I believed illiteracy was part of it, which was why receiving an education was so crucial to me. Nika understood that, and she was also a strong woman of faith who came along at the right time in my life, when God was at work in me. She helped the seeds of my faith continue to grow.

Nika and I began dating, and despite the difficulties at the start of my college career, I believed that attending Lee University was the best thing that could have happened to me.

Coach Moyo had taken a chance on me and had fought for me, and I wanted to build a legacy for both myself and my coach. On top of my spiritual, academic, and athletic successes in college, I had not abandoned my dream of playing professionally, and playing at Lee actually turned that dream into a possibility.

PLAYING PROFESSIONALLY

During my third and final year of college, I was invited as one of one hundred twenty players to the Major League Soccer Player Combine. Lee University wasn't a large school, so no one was really looking at me during the combine. I played very well though, and was drafted by the Columbus Crew Major League Soccer team in January 2008, the second international player to be taken and the twenty-second pick overall.

My dream of playing professional soccer was finally a reality!

I negotiated with Columbus Crew to be able to finish my last semester of college, so I would have a degree. My desire to complete my education had remained strong. I joined the professional soccer team for the first time in Florida for the pre-season during my spring break. The coach was happy to have me there, because it gave both him and the press a chance to see how I fit into the team. And fortunately, I played well in the pre-season matches.

I returned to school for the summer term and finished my college education in three and a half years, graduating cum laude with a major in business. It was a proud moment for me. I was the first person in my family who graduated with a university degree from America.

My parents were not able to attend my graduation at Lee, but they made sure I knew how proud they were. My entire family had always believed in my intelligence. I talked to my parents on the phone shortly after graduation day and could tell how excited they were. Despite me having more money than him at the time, my father told me he would buy me some food when I came to visit. That is the tradition in Haiti. My mother told me she would cook my favorite meal the next time I came home. I was so grateful to be able to share my success with my family and know they were happy for me.

I met back up with the Columbus Crew in late June, after I graduated. It was amazing to finally be a professional player, traveling and living the dream. I loved being on the field, but even outside our matches, life was pure joy. I was traveling to different parts of America, and getting paid to play the game I loved. Columbus was definitely a soccer town, home to the first soccer stadium in the United States.

Fans would come out to see the games, and kids would line up for autographs afterwards. I loved talking to the kids and watching their faces light up as they met professional soccer players.

In 2008, the year I was drafted, my team won the MLS Cup and we were invited to the White House to meet President

Barack Obama. It seemed like I'd finally made my dreams come true.

But things change quickly in the world of professional soccer, and the next year, Columbus Crew had a new coach and new staff. The team decided to cut my contract after I got injured and would have to sit out for part of the season.

The following soccer season, I joined a faith-based team in Cleveland, Ohio, called the City Stars. But at the end of my first season with the City Stars, the team disbanded.

It was 2010 and Nika and I had just gotten married. We were on our honeymoon when I found out that I wouldn't be playing with the City Stars anymore.

I received an offer to play for the Tampa Bay Rowdies in the United Soccer League, but by that time, Nika had been accepted into a graduate school in Cleveland. I declined Tampa Bay's offer, and while Nika went to school, I began working at an Enterprise rental car business. Growing up in Haiti had prepared me for working long hours, and I used my time at Enterprise to learn how to run a successful business. I also began coaching youth soccer clubs, discovering a new love for training the next generation.

Working in an office environment and getting involved with youth soccer players inspired some new dreams in me during these years. Also, at this point in our lives, Nika and I wanted to start a family and settle down a bit. I knew that a soccer career couldn't accommodate our family. A career in soccer has a short lifespan, with most players retiring by their early thirties because they can't keep up with the younger players.

So, in 2010 at age twenty-six, I officially retired from professional soccer.

It might seem like the end of a dream, but I had played soccer for the opportunities it brought me, not just for the career.

SOCCER TOOK ME AROUND THE WORLD, LIFTED ME OUT OF POVERTY, AND HELPED ME GAIN AN EDUCATION IN AMERICA.

As my soccer career came to an end, I started to envision a new path, one that had started years before while I was at Lee University.

CHAPTER EIGHT

HOPE FOR LIFE

During a college break in 2007, I had traveled back to Haiti to spend time with my family. One day, a young boy started following me around Léogâne. When I had lived in Haiti, it was easier to ignore the beggar children on the street, but being at Lee had reshaped my soul, and it was impossible not to see these children now.

This particular boy reminded me of myself when I was younger.

"Ton! Ton!" he would call out. "Give me some money so I can buy food!"

Ton meant uncle, and while he followed me down that street, it struck me that this young boy could easily have been me if I had not had an education and the opportunities it brought. I remembered following the American soldiers around when I was a child, thinking they were Jesus.

"Come here," I told him, and he quickly came up to me. He told me his name was T-Paul.

"Why are you hungry?"

"My parents don't have enough money to feed me," he said.

People in town told me not to listen to him, that he was a beggar and was there every day. I know from experience that it's easy to stop seeing the intense need when it's normal and widespread. I had lived within it for many years. A hungry young beggar is easy to ignore if you allow yourself to become blinded to him.

But I couldn't stop thinking that he could have been me. I was reminded how Jesus looked after the poor, and because of my faith, I wanted to do that as well.

T-Paul was in terrible condition. His shirt was full of holes, and he had no pants. He was filthy, with every inch of him covered in dirt.

"Come with me," I said. I wasn't going to give him money; instead, I was going to buy him something to eat. I took his hand and we began walking to a restaurant. People wondered what I was doing, but I remembered back to my own childhood—how older kids would take my hand when I was young so that I could get to school safely.

I held T-Paul's hand tighter.

When we arrived at the restaurant, they said they would let me in, but not T-Paul.

"You can't come in here with these types of kids," they said. "It will hurt our business."

I was insistent that we both should be served, and so they went to get the restaurant manager. When he came out, the manager recognized me right away. He was excited about having a soccer star in his restaurant, and both T-Paul and I sat down.

After we ate, I took T-Paul back to his home. I asked him why he wasn't in class since it was the middle of a school day.

"My parents don't pay for school," he told me. "They can't afford it."

I still couldn't shake the feeling that I easily could have ended up exactly the same as this young boy. I asked if I could go meet his mother. When she saw us approach, she didn't recognize me. She assumed I was a stranger, and that her son had gotten into trouble.

"What did you do?" she yelled at him.

I assured her that her son wasn't in trouble. "He told me he can't go to school," I said.

In Haiti, people don't want to show a stranger that they are struggling. In our culture, it is considered showing weakness, and so I had upset T-Paul's mother when I told her what he'd said. She was angry that I knew of their financial struggles.

"He's a liar," she said. "He's in school! Don't listen to him."

But I knew the culture. I knew what was going on.

"I just want to help him," I replied. "I saw him, and he's obviously not in school."

Still, T-Paul's mother refuted everything I said. It wasn't that she was arguing with me, or trying to be rude, but she was embarrassed. I understood. I knew she probably felt like a failure, and that was difficult for a parent.

As we continued to talk, the conversation calmed down a bit. I told her who I was, and that was when she recognized me at last.

"I am so sorry!" she said, now embarrassed to have argued with a soccer celebrity.

That's when she opened up, and began to tell her story and her family's struggles. I found out that all T-Paul needed to go to school was ten dollars a month. That amount would cover his uniform and fees, and leave a little money left over.

"No problem," I told her. "I want to help."

I gave her a little money that day, and also gave her my phone number, telling her to call when she needed help. At the time, I truly felt like I could make a change in one young boy's life.

I went back to Lee when vacation was over, and my class studies quickly overwhelmed me again. Being back in my clean, air-conditioned apartment with plenty of food from the grocery store made it easy to push T-Paul out of my mind. Shortly after, I began getting phone calls from T-Paul's mother. I had a lot of assignments, and I was trying to get ready for the MLS Combine, so initially I avoided answering her calls. She persisted, and one day I finally picked up.

"Hello Ricardo," she said. "I wanted to find out if you could help me send T-Paul back to school?" They didn't have the money to send him, so he was going to miss out on starting the new school year.

I told her I would try.

The reality was that I was so busy, and the hassle of figuring out how to send the money through Western Union to get it to T-Paul's mother meant that at first, I just couldn't do it. I didn't have the time. T-Paul wasn't at the front of my mind. My studies and soccer were.

Then one night, I had a dream. It was as if God reminded me of all of the opportunities he had given to me. He was saying that I was chosen to help; that I could have been like T-Paul, that my brother *was* like T-Paul, and my sister was almost like him too.

I woke up convicted, and sure that God was calling me to help.

I couldn't call T-Paul's mother back, because the number she had used was not hers. I called a friend in Haiti instead, and asked him to help me find T-Paul and his family. I gave him the best information I had, telling him about the restaurant and general location.

And then I asked one more thing of my friend: find some other kids like T-Paul too.

THE START OF HOPE

My friend found seven kids, including T-Paul, and I began sending seventy dollars each month to help them go to school. Money was tight for me while I was at Lee, but I knew it was the right thing to do.

> *I HAD UNDERSTOOD GOD'S MESSAGE THAT I WAS CHOSEN TO HELP.*

My friend became an advocate for what I was doing, and during the years I played professionally with Columbus Crew, our education assistance program grew to thirty-five children receiving tuition for school in Haiti. I really felt like I was investing in these kids, helping them get an opportunity and a better chance in life.

And then, on January 12, 2010, everything changed.

The world watched in horror as a massive 7.0 magnitude earthquake shook Haiti to its core.

Léogâne, my hometown, was near the epicenter of the earthquake. Aftershocks rumbled for weeks, many greater than 4.5 magnitude. At least 220,000 people were killed, 1.5 million were displaced, and hundreds of thousands of homes and businesses were destroyed. Historic government buildings collapsed and crumbled. Schools and hospitals pancaked onto themselves, crushing people inside. Images began to emerge, showing my hometown to be little more than a pile of concrete rubble, with rebar jutting out from what had once been familiar buildings.

It was almost impossible to believe what I was seeing, and what the news reports from the disaster were saying. My first concern was my family. I was anxious until I was able to learn that my parents and siblings were all alive and hadn't been hurt. Unfortunately, that wasn't the case for many of my friends in Haiti, who had been hurt or killed.

The friend who had been helping me sponsor the children was unhurt, but he told me that many of the children who we had been helping had died, crushed underneath the poorly built school buildings I had paid to send them to.

I was angry. Angry that they had died, and angry that my three-year investment in their future was wasted because they were buried under cheaply built concrete schools.

My childhood friend, Jean-Robert, helped me find a path forward. He'd experienced the loss of his niece during the earthquake. He saw his sister hold that little girl's dead body, watched her sobbing and begging to be with her daughter, wherever she was. He understood the pain of loss and confusion, but also knew that there were kids who would need more help than ever after the earthquake.

"Pierre-Louis," he said to me, "what you can do is expand that program and help more kids."

I realized he was right. I made sure my family was taken care of, and began sending money to help other people who needed it.

In 2010, six months after the earthquake, I returned to Haiti on a mission trip with OneHope ministries. The purpose of the trip was to use soccer to give hope to kids who had been displaced by the earthquake. In 2013, I went to another region of Haiti called Verrettes *[Vèr-rèt]*, with an organization called Ambassador Sports International, where I was able to play soccer with some of the local kids.

Inevitably, crowds found me, and I was pressed on all sides by people asking for my help. The needs and requests of all these people were overwhelming, and it was not long before I became exhausted. I could not possibly help all of them, but what I was already giving seemed too small to make any real impact. I tried to help some people eat for a day, but I was not giving them any lasting opportunities. And the people I was not able to help wondered why I had not chosen them.

I felt lost and guilty, like I was failing.

In the midst of all this, a man named Berthony Duvelsaint approached me and asked if I would help him with an adult first-division soccer team in Verrettes. I listened to him because he was highly regarded in the community, and a good friend of mine had told me Mr. Duvelsaint was trustworthy. I told him I would like to work with him, but I was not going to help the adults.

"You know with the adults, there is no real opportunity," I told him. "I can help you if you will start a youth soccer academy."

I saw a faint opportunity through soccer for children who still had life ahead of them, who still had hope for a better future. Duvelsaint agreed with my idea, but there was no such thing as a youth soccer club in Verrettes, so we parted ways with no real plans for the future, hoping that someday, somehow, we could work together. Truly, we could not have dreamed of what God had planned.

MAGIC SOCCER

After that trip, Nika and I moved to Bismarck, North Dakota, to be closer to her family. She had completed her physician assistant program in Ohio. But I had a decision to make: I could find another job in the business world and pursue wealth, or try something new. After my experiences with the children in Haiti and coaching youth soccer in the US, I decided to further my education.

It was the next generation that renewed my hope. I saw a future in teaching and coaching youth, showing them how to be global-minded citizens and good people. I wanted to do more than show them how to kick a ball. I wanted to make sure they became young people who were able to embrace opportunity. In order to accomplish that, I knew I needed to become a teacher.

But going to graduate school in America was hard.

Our family was growing, with two baby boys who wouldn't sleep, while I was trying to get my assignments done for my master's degree. Many mornings I was up at 5:00 a.m., studying and entertaining a two-year-old at the same time. Even with the tough balance between work, family, and school, I graduated with honors and received my master's degree in Business and Marketing Education from the University of Mary in Bismarck, North Dakota.

I remember the day I officially became a teacher. For the first time, I felt truly equipped to fulfill my purpose. I remembered many years ago, when I held my father's hand, helping him to write his name. I remembered teaching my mother how to read and write. The connections from the past to that moment were clear.

Soon, I took on a job as a part-time French teacher, then began teaching some business classes as well. By my second year of teaching, I had a full-time teaching position in the public school system and was developing my own teaching philosophy: before I can teach my students, I have to have a relationship and connection with them. I respect them. They respect me. It makes what I teach them that much more valuable.

It was during this time, in 2014, that I also started Magic Soccer FC, an official youth soccer club in Bismarck. Soccer had been my vehicle of opportunity, changing my life and making me who I am today. I saw the same opportunities for the kids in Bismarck. With soccer, they would learn about mental toughness, discipline, and teamwork. My goal was to use soccer to shape youth into global citizens who understood the struggles that others face across the world.

Just after starting Magic Soccer FC in Bismarck, I received a call from Haiti. I usually did not answer unrecognized Haitian numbers because I received dozens of requests for money every month, but for some reason I answered this one. It was Berthony Duvelsaint. He told me he had quit his job working with adult soccer teams to start a youth soccer academy, and he wanted to know if I would still help.

Our moment had come, and I immediately said yes! Through our partnership, we created Magic Soccer Academy Verrettes, which offers elite level soccer training to the youth of Verrettes and the surrounding areas.

The goal of Magic Soccer in Verrettes was to attract kids to greater opportunities through soccer. Students who could not afford school would have my help with the fees, and they would learn the valuable physical and mental skills soccer had to offer. But more importantly, they would learn true hope through the gospel of Jesus Christ, which the coaches in Verrettes would share with them.

The education I helped them pay for would allow them to read and understand the Bible, their life, and society as a whole much better.

WE WANTED THEM TO DEVELOP
INTO GOOD CITIZENS OF
CHARACTER, A TRUE ASSET FOR
THE FUTURE OF HAITI.

Magic Soccer Academy Verrettes also led to the birth of a larger vision, called Lespwa Lavi *[Les-pwah Lah-vee]*. And this is the plan I believe God had in mind all along. Through every game, test, and setback, He was preparing me—and our team and partners—to bring true hope to Haiti.

LESPWA LAVI, HOPE FOR LIFE

I began to realize how broken Haiti's education system is while completing my master's degree in education. I understood that the intense competition to survive Haiti's education system created self-serving attitudes and deep character flaws in Haitian youth from a young age. Memorization drills and corporal punishment for missed answers damaged children in a way that destroyed their hope instead of building it. Pain was all that waited on the other side of failure, rather than another chance to learn and grow. If I could foster globally minded youth in my classroom in Bismarck, North Dakota, why couldn't I do the same in Haiti?

I spoke with others who worked in education and I prayed for guidance. And because of my faith, I felt God showing me that the miracle journey he'd led me on, from poverty to success, was far from over. Throughout my life, God had uniquely prepared me to start a new kind of school in Haiti, a school that would help change the culture of education there. To accomplish such an enormous vision would require the power of an almighty God, one who had proven Himself to me a thousand times over. Every time the world dropped a roadblock in my way throughout my life, God used it to point me toward a greater purpose. He took every obstacle and struggle and created something new and powerful. I also knew this project would take many allies. So I gathered a group of friends with expertise in various professional backgrounds, and we began laying out a vision for Lespwa Lavi Academy.

Lespwa Lavi means "Hope for Life" in Haitian Creole. Mr. Duvelsaint, who I trusted and respected, had done an excellent job running Magic Soccer Academy Verrettes for the last couple years, and so in 2016 I asked him to partner with me in starting Lespwa Lavi Academy in Verrettes.

Verrettes is located in one of the poorest regions of Haiti, a place where few aid organizations arrive. Most people there live on less than $1.25 a day, and they don't know where their next meal will come from. The literacy rate for girls is about 47 percent, and their high school graduation rate is only 1 percent. Boys manage a little bit better with a graduation rate of 2 percent.

Magic Soccer Academy Verrettes had already laid the foundation for change. Our coaches developed the first girls' soccer team in the region. Starting with just ten players, we grew to over one hundred girls playing for Magic Soccer. Other teams in the region started and together they formed a girls' league. As one of the most successful girls' soccer programs in the country, our Magic Soccer girls are recognized and sponsored by FIFA. Many of our girls have graduated high school and gone on to college, or become coaches for Magic Soccer, becoming leaders in their own community.

Duvelsaint agreed that better education was the key to unlocking opportunity, and he shared our vision for the Lespwa Lavi Academy with the community of Verrettes. They immediately donated a parcel of land on a mountain overlooking the city, with just one condition: *we must also build a church.*

THE PROMISED LAND

There's something you must understand about Haiti. It is an island nation roughly equal to the size of Maryland. Not only is land scarce in Haiti, it's also ancestral. It gets passed down from family to family; usually without any legal documentation. So land is neither given up, nor acquired, easily—except when it comes to the government. They can take land whenever they want; even violently. One of my grandparents was killed in a land dispute with the government.

On top of this, there is voodoo land, traditional sites used for ceremonies of darkness. Mountains are especially sacred. You can feel the death and evil in these places. You simply don't go there.

With this in mind, you can imagine our shock when the community of Verrettes donated six acres to us less than a month after we announced the plans for a school. We also learned that one of the community elders had experienced a vision of Lespwa Lavi Academy. He prophesied it would be "a light on the hill; a light to the community."

After that, a poor man named Moise, who lived next to the land, cleared away all of the brush and garbage to prepare for the construction of the church and the academy. Soon after, the town came together and built a little church out of sticks and mud. They said, "If this academy is going to happen, then God has to do it." Then they decided we probably needed even more land. So they donated another six acres for the permanent church site to be built![2]

2. You can read more about the church at https://lespwalavi.org/ministry

Their gift of precious land reminded me of Psalm 135:12, "And He gave their land as an inheritance, an inheritance to his people." In the Old Testament living in *the Promised Land* was part of God's deal with His people. And I felt like He was making the same promise to Lespwa Lavi.

The first time I brought Nika to Verrettes to see our land, she experienced what it's really like to travel in Haiti. We drove for three hours over deep pot-holes, swerving around broken down cars and debris. It was so bad, one ten-mile stretch took forty-five minutes. Another thing to understand is that many villages don't have electricity. After sunset, everything is dark. But as we approached Verrettes, we saw a bright light on the edge of the mountain ahead of us.

I leaned over to Nika and said, "That's our land. They must be having church."

The next morning we found out that there had been all-night prayer services for a week ahead of our arrival. Every night, people had gathered in the church building asking God to break down the voodoo strongholds around the land. Because there was no electricity, a truck had pulled a portable generator with a spotlight attached to a flagpole to light up the prayer meeting every night.

The location of this land mattered because it was a traditional voodoo ceremonial site *and* home to some of the poorest people in the country.

Just like the land God prepared for Israel, I knew our land was special. Even though there are a dozen other mountains, land becomes significant when God attaches a promise to it. Theology professor Chris Bruno writes: "The land is ultimately not just about a place to set up borders or to mark out territory in distinction from a bunch of other countries. The land is a place where God dwells with his people."

Land that God sets aside is a place of promise, peace, and rest. And if there's anything that will bring hope to Haiti, it's for God to dwell there! We knew that occupying a piece of traditional voodoo land would come with more roadblocks. But taking back ground for God's purpose is just another opportunity for Him to show His glory.

On Sunday morning we took our first walk through our Promised Land. We hiked up the side of the mountain where a lone palm tree grew. It was the only survivor of years of overgrazing and deforestation. Some scrawny goats were digging around, looking for something green to eat. From under the palm tree, we looked over the Artibonite Valley below, imagining the school buildings springing up from the limestone. However, as our team of engineers and architects surveyed the land, they realized that the flat area was not wide enough for a soccer field.

As you've learned, soccer is like a religion in Haiti. This is why it's a key part of Lespwa Lavi's vision. This geographical issue was such a problem we talked late into the night about whether or not to search for a new plot of land. After some

measurements, we found that if we added just thirty meters to the acreage, there would be enough flat space to build the field. But this roadblock seemed insurmountable—someone else owned the adjacent land, and because he lived in Canada, no one knew how to reach him.

Our team prayed that night, knowing this land had been gifted as a promise, but we still didn't know what to do. The next morning, Duvelsaint and I began looking for a way to contact the owner to somehow buy the extra thirty meters. Miraculously, he just happened to be visiting that day from Canada! It turned out he was the chief surveyor in that district. So not only did he own most of the land in Verrettes, he was the only person authorized to sign it over with legal documentation. I visited his office to talk to him about buying the land, but at first he ignored me and continued with his work. I didn't know what else to do, so I told him about our church on the hill, and that we were Christians. This was a gamble, because he could have negative opinions toward Christians. However, the man stopped what he was doing and looked Duvelsaint and I over.

He got up and walked to the other room, where he made a phone call to Canada. We waited, knowing he was speaking with other family members who had rights to the land. We had no idea if we should wait or leave.

After several minutes, the man returned, sat down, narrowed his eyes, and leaned across the table. "I've watched this community struggle and fail for my entire life," he said. "Here's what I will do. I will give you the land, but not because of you. Because of the Kingdom of God."

He signed over the land right then and there!

After that successful meeting, our faith grew even more. I wholeheartedly believe that when God attaches a promise to land, it becomes significant, and miracles happen one after another.

> *LESPWA LAVI MEANS "HOPE FOR LIFE," AND WE DO INTEND TO BE A LIGHT ON THE HILL, GUIDING THE YOUTH OF HAITI OUT OF DARKNESS.*

We continue to plan the Lespwa Lavi campus and pray against the spiritual giants in the land—the corruption and darkness that wants to keep God's Kingdom from taking hold. But just like Jesus told Peter in Matthew 16:18, "I will build my church, and the gates of hell shall not prevail against it."

I'm happy to say Jesus is still building His church. Today, two hundred people now attend that church in a region known for

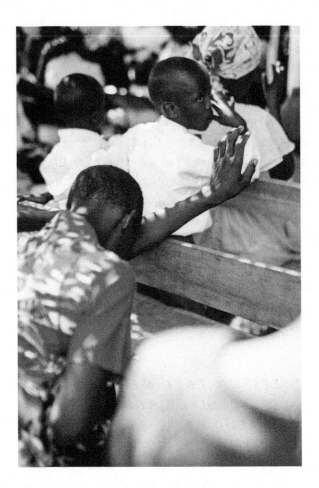

its voodoo practices and animist religion. And the Lespwa Lavi
congregation has been instrumental in the hopeful revival in
the community.

We partnered with Engineering Ministries International
(EMI) to design an earthquake and hurricane resistant
campus, because I did not want to relive the nightmare of
buildings collapsing and killing my students. We developed a
phased plan for construction, starting with the church, school
buildings, and soccer field. In the future, we plan to add a
medical clinic, guesthouse, and additional school buildings.

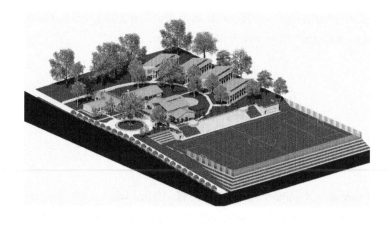

At the beginning of 2019, we launched a child advocacy program that provided for the basic needs of children. Through this program, the children in Verrettes have access to nutrition, clean water, medical care, education, and a mentor or advocate who shares Christ with them and monitors their growth and safety. In order to make this program sustainable, we partnered with the organization Convoy of Hope to launch a daily nutrition program. Over three hundred children have been fed every day through this partnership, and they no longer have to suffer from waterborne illnesses. The nutrition and advocacy program started just in time to respond to the Haitian political crisis of 2019 and the COVID-19 health crisis in 2020, when Haiti was brought to the brink of starvation.

TO TRULY HAVE HOPE,
HAITIANS NEED TO HAVE
OPPORTUNITY.

I'd received a good education in Haiti, but what really led me to success wasn't that schooling, but soccer. It was soccer that took me around the world. It was soccer that led me to an American university.

In order to create opportunity, Lespwa Lavi Academy is different from the traditional Haitian education system. Our curriculum creates a dual path to success, through academic achievement and athletic development. Critical and independent thinking skills are the core of our academy— skills that are completely absent in Haiti's state curriculum. Foundational to our success is that students will also learn English so they can compete in every possible way outside of Haiti.

With this foundation, students can take college entrance exams anywhere in the world. Their athletic skills will open doors to athletic scholarships.

Our goal is to provide an open door for students so that after finishing school, they can find jobs and have opportunities to keep going. We want to help students become entrepreneurs, innovators, and global citizens who are aware of how they fit into their country, and how their country fits into the world. Lespwa Lavi uses soccer to bring the community together and help them help themselves. Through the success of Magic

Soccer Academy Verrettes, soccer has opened the door for the people of Haiti to hear about a different path. When you can speak through soccer, the people are ready to hear about the hope of Christ, and the chance to live for something bigger than oneself.

We can see the waves of hope already changing the landscape of Verrettes and rippling across all of Haiti. While many organizations have come to help in Haiti, they do not always understand the people, our culture, and our traditions. Short-term aid is good, but it doesn't have lasting effects. We need more than a meal; we need a path to opportunity.

Haitians know best what Haiti needs.

It is difficult for outside cultures to understand what soccer is for Haiti. As you've read, soccer is empowerment and opportunity. It has the ability to move people and change situations. Soccer is a game of peace, and when there's unity, anything is possible.

Together, we can take the hands of millions of kids, and feed them more than hope. We can help them create their future. Together, we can provide jobs and scholarships to help kids get an education they'd never receive otherwise.

In Haiti, life itself is a competition, and its people are some of the world's fiercest competitors.

We are giving these children a chance on that playing field.

CONCLUSION

You are like me, I think, in that you want to make a positive difference in the world. It's a big world though, and it's not always clear how one person can be or do anything significant enough to make the world better.

But just like you win a soccer match one goal at a time, you change the world one child at a time.

My story is one of opportunity, about how people created opportunities for me, and made sacrifices to make the way easier for me. Every life I've had the opportunity to influence is credited to those who have helped me. Like a tree, one child grows, branches out, helps children who come after them, and they continue the pattern.

That can still happen. The tree is still growing.

Soccer was my path of opportunity, and creating a path to better futures for more children is my purpose and my greatest hope. With your help, we can continue the work. For $38 each month, you can change the world one child at a time by making sure they have good food, clean water, and an education.

The future will change for your sponsored child, their family, their community, and for Haiti. And I have no doubt that you will see your own life changed as well.

Find out more about child sponsorships on our website at: lespwalavi.org/childsponsorships

ACKNOWLEDGMENTS

I want to thank God most of all, because without Him, I wouldn't be able to do any of this.

Writing a book is harder than I thought and more rewarding than I could have ever imagined. None of this would have been possible without my beautiful wife, Nika. Thank you for your ongoing support over the years, and your tireless nights editing and bringing my story to life. And...thank you for taking care of Rocco, Caleb, Luca and the soon-to-be-born while I took time writing this book in our basement.

Writing a book about the story of your life is a surreal process. I'm forever indebted to Jordan Loftis and his wife Joelle, their publishing company, Story Chorus, Anna Thompson, and Ashton Hauff. I am thankful for their editorial help, keen insight, amazing cover design, and ongoing support in bringing my story into life. It is because of their gifts, efforts and encouragement that I have been able to tell this powerful story. Their aid in writing this story has helped me bring hope and change to the people of Haiti, and helped the rest of the world understand the power of soccer.

Thank you to John and Maria Dwyer and Dr. Mike Taylor who took the chance to travel to Haiti for the first time with a stranger. The world is a better place thanks to people who develop, mentor, lead, and trust God. What makes it even better are people who share the gift of their time, their resources, and their hearts to help others. Thank you for mentoring me, helping me grow, and supporting my fellow Haitians.

To my college coach at Lee University, Henry Moyo, for bringing me to the United States in the pursuit of better opportunities. He never saw my race, or my lack of English speaking skills. He just saw a young soccer player, hungry to learn, hungry to grow, and hungry for a better life. He never stopped paving the road of opportunity for me.

Retiring from professional soccer was one of the hardest things I have endured. Soccer was the only thing I knew; soccer was everything to me. Although the period of my life after soccer was filled with many ups and downs, my father-in-law helped me understand life beyond soccer. Sometimes fathers-in-law can be scary, but Joel Puffe was a real father. He was a prophet in my life. He consoled me, helped me grow spiritually, mentored me, and rescued me. It wouldn't have been possible for me to be the strong follower of Jesus that I am today without Joel as my spiritual leader.

Without the love and support from my family over the years, this book would not exist. I want to thank my maman Gislene J Pierre-Louis, and my siblings Delma Joinville, Ansdher Civil, Roosevelt Civil, Nancy Pierre-Louis, Yves-Andre Pierre-Louis, and Daphney Pierre-Louis.

Finally, I am thankful for Berthony Duvelsaint, the board of Lespwa Lavi, the community of Bismarck, North Dakota, the Magic Soccer Academy players and parents, and all of our donors. Thank you for being the inspiration and foundation of hope and change to the people of Haiti.

ABOUT THE AUTHOR

Ricardo was born in Léogâne, Haiti. He moved to the United States in 2004 to play college soccer on a scholarship. In 2008, Ricardo graduated from Lee University (TN) with a bachelor's degree in Business Administration. Ricardo earned his master's degree in Business Education at the University of Mary (ND). Ricardo has been a licensed business and marketing teacher at Bismarck High School since 2017.

At Lee University, Ricardo was a three time Collegiate Soccer All American, National Player of the year, and Academic All American. He scored 101 goals in 69 games and holds the all time scoring record at Lee. After his career, his jersey number 19 was retired and Ricardo was inducted to the Lee University Hall of Fame.

Ricardo was drafted in the second round (the twenty-second pick) by the Columbus Crew in the MLS super draft. He was part of the Crew team who won the 2008 MLS Cup, as well as the Supporter Shield Cup. Ricardo also played for the Haitian National Team for nine years. He had 48 caps with the senior national team. He has played in major tournaments for Haiti like the Gold Cup, World Cup Qualifying, and the Carribean Cup. During his time with the Haitian National Team, he had the opportunity to play against the world's best soccer players, like Landon Donovan, David Beckam, Ronaldinho Gaucho, and Ronaldo Luis Nazario. Ricardo's most cherished soccer moment was playing against the five-time world cup champion Brazilian soccer team.

Ricardo started playing soccer at age three in the streets of Léogâne, where soccer was the only way out. When he was twelve , the local club youth coach invited him for a trial with the academy, and that simple act changed his life forever. He never stopped playing, and after moving to the US, Ricardo developed an interest in youth soccer coaching. For over twelve years Ricardo has touched the lives of countless youths of various ages through the beautiful game of soccer. Ricardo is the owner and founder of Magic Soccer FC, a successful youth soccer academy in North Dakota.

Ricardo has been married to Nika, a North Dakota native, since 2009. The couple have three sons, Rocco, Caleb, and Luca, and are currently expecting their fourth child.

ABOUT LESPWA LAVI

Founded in 2013, Lespwa Lavi means "Hope for Life" in Haitian Creole. What began as a youth soccer academy in the rural Artibonite region of Haiti has grown into a mission to empower the community of Verrettes and create a sustainable, impactful ministry with four main goals:

- To equip and prepare students to transform their community and the world for the glory of Jesus Christ

- To provide an environment for all soccer players to achieve their potential

- Meet basic community needs in the poorest region of Haiti

- Unite the communities of Verrettes and Bismarck, ND and other communities in the United States

Haitian agronomist and community leader, Berthony Duvelsaint approached former Haitian National Team and Major League Soccer player, Ricardo Pierre-Louis, in 2013 in order to create a youth soccer development program. Mr. Duvelsaint is a native of Verrettes, which is a very poor rural farming community in the notorious Artibonite region of Haiti. Together they started the first girls' team in the region, which has garnered international attention. The soccer program uses the popular game to create mentorships between players and coaches and provides scholarships for students to attend school. The coaches ensure students are attending school, that their nutritional and medical needs are being met, and they lead weekly Bible studies.

As the soccer program grew successfully, Ricardo felt that God was leading him to start a school that would provide opportunity for Haitian children to fulfill their dreams. In 2016, plans were formulated to create Lespwa Lavi Academy, a bilingual modern school that will prepare students for a university level education.

The community of Verrettes heard about this dream and donated 15 acres of land for the Academy to be built. The community leaders prophesied that if the Academy is going to be successful, God has to do it. So, they started a church! In 2017, Assemblee de Dieu des Verrettes was founded and plays a key role in paving the way for Lespwa Lavi. The church is supported by a community partner church in the United States.

In 2019, Lespwa Lavi hosted its first medical and dental mission trip, partnering with Haitian nurses and medical students. The lack of access to primary care was evident, and as a result of that trip, Lespwa Lavi formed a partnership with a local facility in the nearby town of Marin to begin providing consistent primary care soon. Plans are underway to design the first facility in Verrettes that will provide primary medical care and dental care.

Learn more at: **www.lespwalavi.org**